DICTIONARIES OF WORLD RELIGIONS

ISLAM

Richard Tames

B.T. Batsford Limited   London

First published 1985
Reprinted 1987

Typeset by Tek-Art Ltd, Kent
and printed in Great Britain by
R.J. Acford Ltd,
Chichester, Sussex
for the publishers
B.T. Batsford Ltd,
4 Fitzhardinge Street
London W1H 0AH

ISBN 0 7134 3655 7

Acknowledgments

The Author and Publishers thank the following for their kind permission to reproduce copyright illustrations: Barnaby's Picture Library, pages 23, 46, 53; The Institute of Isma'ili Studies Ltd, page 37; IPA Picture Library, pages 43, 48; Keystone Press Agency Ltd, pages 31, 58, 63; Wendy Livesey, page 38; The Mansell Collection Ltd, pages 4, 24 (bottom), 56 (bottom); Christine Osborne, pages 6, 10, 15, 20, 22 (bottom), 27 (bottom), 28, 29, 41, 59, 60; Topham Picture Library, pages 44, 54. The map on page 18 was drawn by R.F. Brien. All other illustrations in the book are copyright of the Author. The pictures were researched by Patricia Mandel.

Cover pictures

The colour photograph on the front cover shows Evening prayer in the Badshahi Mosque in Lahore (Christine Osborne). The left-hand picture shows stucco panels on the walls of a seventeenth-century mosque and college in Kairouan, Tunisia (Richard Tames); and the right-hand picture shows Pakistanis leaving Karachi by ship for Mecca, on the annual *Haj* ship "Shams" (Christine Osborne).

Introduction

Islam is the religion of at least one sixth of the world's population, perhaps more, for its followers, Muslims, are growing in numbers, by natural increase and by conversion, every year. Muslims form the majority population in some fifty countries, stretching right across the world from Morocco to Indonesia, as well as being the largest non-Christian community in Europe.

Living in cities and villages, barren mountains and fertile plains, working as farmers or craftsmen or government officials, Muslims show and experience great diversities of human condition, diversities of wealth and of health and of knowledge. But practising Muslims would affirm that the diversity is nothing beside the unity of believers, worshipping God and following the teachings of his Prophet Muhammad, as revealed in the Qur'an.

Islam, as any Muslim will tell you, is much more than "just a religion", if, by a religion, we simply mean a set of private beliefs and rituals set aside for special times and places. Islam to its followers is a "*din*", a complete way of life, embracing worship, morals and doctrine; governing the believer's relations not only with God but also with nature and society; it is a culture, a civilization, a world-view. This book is an introduction to that world-view.

A Note on Spelling

There is no generally accepted way of spelling Arabic words and names in English. For this reason, you are likely to come across the same word or name spelt in different ways in different books (e.g. Koran – Qur'an; Mohammed – Muhammad). In this book we have chosen to use the simplest form in most general use. Common alternative spellings are also indicated in many entries. Because the form of transliteration has been greatly simplified, it should not be taken as an accurate guide to pronunciation. The *ayn*, written ' , has been retained in the middle of words, where it marks a pause between syllables.

Qur'an References

The Qur'an is divided into 114 parts, known as *suras*. Muslims refer to each *sura* by its particular name, but western scholars, for ease of reference, refer to specific passages by the number of the *sura* and the particular verse. These references are given in brackets in many entries in the text. Because different translators divide the verses at different points, the numbers referring to verses may vary slightly from one version to another.

Extracts from the Qur'an (printed in *italics*) have been taken from Arthur J. Arberry, *The Koran Interpreted*, published by Oxford University Press, 1964.

Abbasids

See *Caliphate*.

Ablution

Ablution (*wudu*) is the ritual of washing which a Muslim must perform before offering prayer (5:8). Normally this involves the use of running water, but in cases of necessity sand or even dust can be used. *Wudu* is concerned with the parts of the body exposed to dirt and the public view. The first step is to say that one intends to perform *wudu* and the second to pronounce the *bismillah* ("In the Name of God, the Merciful, the Compassionate"). The hands are washed up to the wrists, then mouth and nostrils are rinsed, after this come the face, forearms, scalp, ears and feet, each action three times. Where there is no water, once is held to be sufficient. Most mosques have a supply of running water so that this duty may be easily performed. A saying attributed to the Prophet is that "Cleanliness is half the faith."

See also *Bismillah, Prayer.*

Muslims at a mosque in Durban, South Africa, prepare themselves for prayer.

Abraham

According to the Qur'an, God revealed the true religion, Islam, first of all to Abraham (in Arabic, Ibrahim), who was therefore the first Muslim (3:67). Abraham and Moses (in Arabic, Musa) are the most frequently mentioned prophets in the Qur'an. The Qur'an also tells that Abraham rejected the worship of the sun, moon and stars and turned to the one creator God. When he believed that God wanted him to sacrifice his beloved son as an act of worship, he was prepared to do so (37:81), but God spared him; and the son, Ishmael, became, according to Muslim tradition, the father of the Arab peoples. The tradition also tells how together, Abraham and Ishmael rebuilt the Ka'ba, after it had been destroyed by the great flood which is also described in the Old Testament.

See also *Hajj, Ka'ba, Prophets*.

> *No; Abraham in truth was not a Jew,*
> *neither a Christian; but he was a Muslim*
> *and one pure of faith; certainly he was never of the*
> *idolaters.*
> *Surely the people standing closest to Abraham*
> *are those who followed him, and this Prophet,*
> *and those who believe; and God is the Protector*
> *of the believers.*
>
> *The House of Imran (3:60).*

Adhan

Adhan is the call to prayer in Islam. The literal meaning of the Arabic word is "announcement". Traditionally, the *adhan* has been given from a minaret (see *Mosque*) by a *muezzin*. Nowadays, tape-recordings and loud-speakers are sometimes used. Using the human voice as a summons to worship distinguishes Muslims from Christians, who use a bell, and Jews, who use a horn.

The call to prayer also declares the most basic beliefs of a Muslim:

> God is most great! (said four times)
> I witness that there is no god but God. (said twice)
> I witness that Muhammad is the Messenger of God. (said twice)
> Come to prayer. (said twice)
> Come to salvation. (said twice)
> (Prayer is better than sleep.) (said twice at dawn prayer)
> God is most great! (said again twice)
> There is no god but God.

The *adhan* should also be repeated in the right ear of a baby as soon as possible after it is born. From its very first moment, a baby should know that prayer is the duty of all believers.

See also *Mosque, Muezzin, Prayer*.

The call to prayer (*adhan*) is usually made from a minaret. This minaret, at Kairouan in Tunisia, dates back to at least the ninth century and is one of the oldest in the world. Note the loudspeakers.

Africa

Congregational mosque in Senegal, West Africa.

Islam came to Northern Africa with the first wave of conquests in the seventh and eighth centuries. But it was merchants and not armies who took it south across the Sahara, by camel caravan to West Africa and by sea to East Africa, lured by the trade in gold, salt and slaves. Gradually, through example and through compromise, Islam was adopted by followers of traditional African religions. In the eighteenth and nineteenth centuries compromises were rejected in West Africa by the followers of reformers like Uthman dan Fodio (1754-1817), who fought a series of *jihads* to establish what he and his followers held to be true, purified Islam. Nevertheless, many people who claimed to be, and thought of themselves as, Muslims at the same time continued to observe such traditions as revering their ancestors and relying on magicians to cure illnesses and bad luck. This was particularly true in rural areas. In the cities, orthodox Islam has always been stronger. Nowadays, Islam is at its strongest in such countries as Nigeria (especially the North), Senegal, Mali and Sudan, though it is also well represented in Ghana, Cameroun, Tanzania and many other African countries. Like Christianity,

Islam continues to gain many converts at the expense of older religious traditions. Architecture, education, politics and social customs all reveal the impact of Islam across the continent.

See also *Ahmadiyya, Folk Religion, Jihad, Slavery.*

A king who protected Muslims or even converted to Islam became part of the international community, giving him considerable advantages over non-Muslim rivals. Literacy (in Arabic), the expansion of trade and even the opportunity to dispossess his non-Muslim neighbours by launching a jihad against them provided the inducement which made Islam an attractive 'royal cult' for many West African princelings.
(Malise Ruthven, *Islam in the World*, Penguin, 1984)

6

Afterlife

Belief in life after death (*akhira*) is a basic doctrine of Islam and one of the aspects of Muhammad's teaching which the Meccan unbelievers rejected most strongly. Muslims believe that death will be followed by a day of judgment when the dead will be called from their tombs by the angel Israfil and the righteous will be separated from the damned by passing over a narrow bridge. The righteous will go on to paradise (*al-janna* – the garden), which is described in the Qur'an as a beautiful garden of eternal delights where true believers will finally experience the presence of God. (The English word "paradise" comes from the Persian word for a walled garden.) The wicked will fall off the bridge and go down to hell (*jahannam*), a place of everlasting fire and torment. Muslim folk religion has made much of the idea that holy men may be able to intercede on behalf of souls facing judgment, but orthodox belief stresses that the believer faces God alone.

See also *Angels, Beliefs, Holy Men, Jerusalem, Jihad, Mahdi*.

Ahmadiyya

A movement founded by Mirza Ghulam Ahmad (1835-1908), born in Qadian in the Punjab, who, after long years of study, believed himself to be a reviver of Islam. He attracted many followers throughout Northern India and what is now Pakistan. His teachings were generally conventional. He argued that mere outward observance of religious duties was useless without sincere belief; he condemned tobacco and also warlike *jihad;* but he upheld polygamy and *purdah*. Controversy followed his death and the movement split in 1914. One group, with its headquarters in Lahore, claimed that the founder was no more than a reformer of Islam and has tried to keep up links with the general community of Islam. The other group shifted its base from Qadian in India when the sub-continent was partitioned in 1947, so that it could be established at Rabwah in Pakistan, a Muslim state. The Rabwah section of the movement holds that the founder was a true prophet. This is a belief quite unacceptable to the mass of Muslims, who hold that Muhammad was the last of all prophets. Both branches of the movement produce a great amount of literature and support well-organized missionary teams in many parts of the world, especially Africa. The Ahmadiyya have, however, been a target for strong opposition in many Muslim communities. In 1974 the government of Pakistan declared the Ahmadiyya to be a non-Muslim minority.

See also *Islam in South Asia, Prophets*.

Foundation stone of the Ahmadiyya mosque in south-west London.

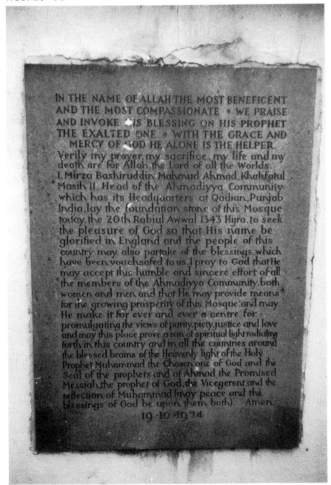

Ali

Ali Ibn Abi Talib was the cousin and son-in-law of the prophet Muhammad and is the most important figure in the development of Shi'ite Islam. Ali became a Muslim as a boy, growing up as a member of Muhammad's family. He married the Prophet's daughter, Fatima, and they had two sons, Hasan and Husayn. A brave warrior and trusted judge and diplomat, he became Caliph in 656, only to have his authority challenged by Muawiyah, Governor of Syria and a member of the powerful Umayyad family. After Ali's assassination (661), Muawiyah took over as Caliph and founded a new dynasty. Ali is buried at al-Najaf, outside Kufa, which he had made his capital and a great seat of learning. His burial place has become an important place of pilgrimage for Shi'ites, some of whom regard Ali as almost equal to the Prophet in piety and wisdom and as a source of guidance.

See also *Caliphate, Imam, Isma'ilis, Shi'ites.*

Allah

Belief in one God is basic to Islam. "Allah" is Arabic for "*the* God". Belief in the "oneness" of God is called, in Arabic, *tawhid*. The main question of belief distinguishing Muslims from Christians is that Muslims cannot accept the idea of God being, at one and the same time, Father, Son and Holy Spirit. Although they accept and revere Jesus as a true prophet sent by God, they reject as "association" (*shirk*, in Arabic) the belief that Jesus is the son of God. Sura 112 states clearly: "Say, he is Allah, the One. Allah is Eternal and Absolute. None is born of Him, nor is He born. And there is none like Him." Muslims believe God to be the creator of the universe and the judge of mankind, all-knowing, all-seeing, all-powerful – but God is also the Compassionate,the Merciful. The duty of a Muslim is to worship God and to accept and obey God's commands, revealed in the Qur'an. All created things depend on God. God depends on nothing and no one.

See also *Beliefs, al-Fatiha, Islam, Jesus, Law.*

God
there is no god but He, the
Living, the Everlasting.
Slumber seizes Him not, neither sleep;
to Him belongs
all that is in the heavens and the earth.
Who is there that shall intercede with Him
save by His leave?
He knows what lies before them
and what is after them,
and they comprehend not anything of His knowledge
save such as He wills.
His throne comprises the heavens and earth;
the preserving of them oppresses Him not;
He is the All-high, the All-glorious.

The Cow (2:256)

The affirmation that God alone is to be worshipped means, for the man of true piety and rigorous sincerity, that no other objective must claim man's effort or loyalty; he must fear no other power, honour no other prize, pursue no other goal. . . . Religion is nowadays sometimes spoken of as man's search for God. On this, the Islamic position is like the Jewish and the Christian, rejecting such a view emphatically, and asserting rather that God takes the initiative. . . . Man's business in the religious life is not a quest but a response.
(Wilfred Cantwell Smith, *The Faith of Other Men*, Canadian Broadcasting Corporation Publications, 1962)

Angels

Angels (*mala'kah*) are mentioned in the Qur'an as God's tireless messengers and servants. They worship God, record the good and bad deeds of men and collect men's souls when they die. Their main task is to link earth-bound man to God. Unlike men, angels have not been given the power to choose freely between good and evil actions. Able only to obey, angels are therefore spared the day of judgment. Most celebrated of the angels are Jibrail (Gabriel), who brought God's revelations to Muhammad; Mikail (Michael), champion of the faith; Izrail, the angel of death; Israfil, who will sound the call to judgment at the ending of the world; and Malik, the master of Hell. Angels need neither to eat nor drink; some Muslims have therefore said that fasting makes men become more like angels and therefore better able to serve God.

See also *Afterlife, Jerusalem.*

Arabic Language

Even before Islam, the Arabs took great pride in their language. Poets were highly honoured among them, partly because they sang the praises of the warriors, women and horses of the tribe to which they belonged, partly for the sheer pleasure their compositions gave the listener. The power of the Qur'an as a form of poetry helps therefore to explain the force of its impact on the Arabs. And poetry continued to be a major part of Arab culture, even after the rise of Islam.

Because Muslims believe the Qur'an to be the literal word of God, they have always taken great care to respect the accuracy of its language. Translations may be made for purposes of study, but acts of worship and forms of prayer depend on the Qur'an in its original Arabic form. Some mastery of Arabic is, therefore, an essential part of the education of every Muslim, and even the most elementary knowledge of Arabic helps to reinforce the sense of unity among Muslims everywhere, whatever the other languages they use in their daily life. It is also noteworthy that such major languages as Farsi (in Iran) and Urdu (in Pakistan) are written in the Arabic script.

The rapid expansion of the Muslim empire in the century after Muhammad's death saw the emergence of Arabic as an international language of learning. Under the Abbasid Caliphs,

Arabic is very much a living language, for commercial as well as religious purposes.

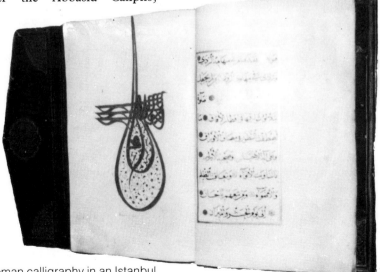

A fine example of Ottoman calligraphy in an Istanbul museum.

Note the numerous different styles of calligraphy in this tile decoration.

translations of Greek, Persian and Indian texts on science and philosophy were made on a systematic basis, by officially sponsored scholars. And it was largely through these translations into Arabic (which were translated in turn into Latin, by Christian and Jewish scholars in Muslim-ruled Spain), that medieval Europe acquired its knowledge of the achievements of the ancient Greeks. For this reason, a great many scientific terms in European languages are derived from Arabic words. In English, for instance, they include "alkali", "alcohol", "zero", "zenith", "benzine" and "algebra".

Another sign of the respect given in Islam to the Arabic language is the importance of Arabic calligraphy in Islamic art and architecture.

See also *Education, Qur'an*.

Architecture and Art

When Islam came to the Arabs, they had a culture rich in poetry but poor in most other respects. Yet, within a couple of centuries, artistic styles which were recognizably "Islamic" had begun to emerge. Drawing on the techniques and materials used by the peoples they conquered in Syria, Persia and elsewhere, the designers and craftsmen employed by Muslim rulers expressed both their power and their piety by constructing massive forts, splendid palaces and magnificent mosques.

The concern of Islam to stamp out the worship of idols and images made pious Muslims hostile to the inclusion of human and animal forms in sculpture or painting, in case they too were worshipped. This disapproval did not, however, entirely prevent the development of such arts as the carving of ivory or the painting of "miniatures" to illustrate story-books and poems; both of these involved human and animal figures, which can also be found on ceramics and metalwork; but these arts were limited to purposes of decoration and illustration, rather than being admired for their own sake. And human and animal motifs were employed only on secular objects and buildings (like palaces) and never on sacred ones like mosques. The contrast with Christianity and Buddhism, which have exalted Christ and Buddha as central figures in their artistic traditions, could not be more marked.

In Islam, therefore, the main tendency of artistic development was towards what might be called abstract and symbolic forms, rather than life-like, naturalistic ones. Three main strands – calligraphy based on Arabic, the sacred language of the Qur'an; plant forms, which suggested the creative power of God; and geometric patterns, which suggest the ideas of infinity and order – were woven together to provide Muslim artists with a repertoire of decorative styles which could be applied to any surface, whether it were the walls of a mosque, a mosaic floor, the cover of a Qur'an or the sleeves of a garment. These distinctive decorative motifs are usually described by the general term "arabesque".

Piety decreed that the arts of the book – calligraphy, manuscript illumination and book-binding – should be supreme in Islam, as most directly of service to the word of God. The practitioners of these arts were therefore the most highly respected. But princely patronage also led to stunning achievements in weaving, jewellery and ceramics, as surviving examples from the courts of the Ottomans, Safavids and Mughals testify.

See also *Bismillah, Crescent, Idolatry, Mosque, Qur'an.*

Roman columns re-used to make an impressive arcade in the Great Mosque at Kairouan, Tunisia. Look at them carefully and you will notice that they are often quite different in style but the overall effect is still harmonious.

Carpet-weaving is not just a "minor art" in the Islamic world.

London's central mosque at Regent's Park was designed by an English architect, Sir Frederick Gibberd.

Stucco, tile and mosaic combine with cool marble and dark woodwork to produce a light but soothing atmosphere in the hallway of this *zawiya* (religious training centre) in Kairouan, Tunisia.

Marble inlay and carved low relief at the Red Fort, Agra.

Islamic art now has an international following and is well-represented in many Western museums and galleries.

The Taj Mahal, perhaps the most famous building in the Islamic world, is not a mosque but a tomb, built in memory of the widow of Shah Jehan, a Mughal emperor of the early seventeenth century.

Astronomy

Muslim interest in the heavens is pre-figured in the Qur'an itself, which makes several references to the stars and planets. But there were practical reasons as well. Not only were astronomical observations extremely useful for caravans travelling by night across trackless wastes of desert; they were also essential for devout believers who wished to know the right direction (*qibla*) for prayer, and also for working out the details of the Islamic calendar with its fasts and festivals. Building on the work of Greek, Persian and Indian pioneers, Muslim astronomers like al-Khwarizmi (d. 846) made many useful observations, with the result that many stars to this day are known by the Arabic names that they gave them. It should be remembered that the original Arabic term, which is translated literally as "the knowledge of the degrees of the stars", covered both astronomy and astrology.

See also *Calendar, Qibla*.

Sundial in the courtyard of the Great Mosque, Kairouan, Tunisia.

Ayatullah

Meaning literally "sign" or "guidance from God", the title of *Ayatullah* is held by the highest religious leaders of the Shi'ite community. Armed with a long training in religious law and doctrine, *ayatullahs* are looked to by the faithful for guidance on both spiritual and worldly matters. An *ayatullah* of forceful personality can become a leader of national and even international significance, as the Ayatullah Khomeini did in Iran. Exiled by the Shah in 1962, he returned to lead a massive civil insurrection which led to the overthrow of the Pahlavi dynasty and the establishment of a self-styled "Islamic Republic", which Khomeini in effect governed by a combination of personal authority and appeals to tradition.

See also *Shi'ites*.

al-Azhar

Al-Azhar (literally "the brilliant") is the greatest single centre of teaching and learning in the Muslim world and is claimed to be one of the oldest anywhere. Founded in 972 by the Fatimid dynasty in Cairo, it originally served as both a mosque and a training centre for Isma'ili missionaries. Later it became a centre for training 'ulama (religious judges) and teachers. In the twentieth century, under the influence of reformers like Muhammad Abduh (1849-1905), who sought to reconcile Islam and western learning, it has come more and more to resemble a western-style university, accepting women students and offering courses not only in law, theology and Arabic but also in a wide range of scientific and technical subjects. The holder of the office of Shaikh al-Azhar, the head of the institution, is widely regarded as an outstanding expert on questions of Islamic belief and practice.

See also *Education, Isma'ilis*.

Al-Azhar, the mosque begun in 969 by the Fatimid dynasty.

Beliefs

The most basic of Muslim beliefs is in the oneness of God, *tawhid*: "Say, He is Allah, the One. Allah is Eternal and Absolute. None is born of Him, nor is He born. And there is none like Him." Coupled with this is an acknowledgment that God's will is supreme throughout the universe, which He alone has created, sustains, guides and will judge. Man's very knowledge of Allah implies belief in His prophets, angels and books – the Qur'an, Gospel (*Injil*), Torah (*Tawrat*) and Psalms (*Zabur*) – through which that knowledge is transmitted and preserved. Belief in the inevitability of the day of judgment and in the reality of life after death in turn imply man's duty of obedience to his creator.

See also *Afterlife, Allah, Angels, al-Fatiha, Prophets, Qur'an.*

> ... loyalty to Islam is expressed, first and foremost, not by correct belief but by correct behaviour – that is, by acceptance of the norms and patterns of Islamic life, loyalty to the Islamic community, and obedience to the head of the Islamic state. Consequently it is deviation from custom, withdrawal from the community, and disobedience to authority, rather than incorrect belief, which constitute the nearest Islamic equivalents of heresy.
> (Bernard Lewis, *Islam from the Prophet Muhammad to the Fall of Constantinople*, Macmillan, 1974)

Bismillah

Also spelt "basmala", this refers to the shortened version of "bismillah al-rahman, al-rahim" – "In the Name of God, the Merciful, the Compassionate." These words begin every *sura* of the Qur'an (except the ninth) and are used by pious Muslims before starting any action, whether it be offering prayer, giving a sermon, eating a meal, joining battle or setting out on a journey. The *bismillah* is also a common motif in Islamic calligraphy and can often be seen written as a protective text on buses and lorries.

See also *Food and Drink.*

> ... the two Divine names, al-rahman and al-rahim ... are derived from the same root rahama. ... Al-Rahman is the transcendent aspect of Divine Mercy. It is a mercy which like the sky envelopes and contains all things. ... As for al-rahim it is the immanent mercy of God. It is like a ray of light which shines in our heart and touches individual lives and particular events. The two qualities combined express the totality of Divine Mercy which envelopes us from without and shines forth from within our being.
> (Seyyed Hossein Nasr, *Ideals and Realities of Islam*, Allen and Unwin, 1966)

Black Muslims

Officially titled "the Nation of Islam", this American religious movement was founded in Detroit by Wallace D. Fard Muhammad (1877-1934) and developed by Elijah Muhammad (1897-1975) and Malcolm X (1925-65) as a vehicle of protest against the disadvantages suffered by black people in the United States. Rejecting Christianity as a "white man's religion", the Black Muslims fastened on to Islam as a faith of power and prestige, deeply rooted in their ancestral homelands. Imposing a stern discipline and high ethical standards on their followers, the Black Muslims diverged from the teachings of the Qur'an in regarding Fard as, in effect, a prophet on a par with Muhammad, in denying the reality of an afterlife and in upholding an attitude of reverse racialism, exalting black people above white rather than regarding all believers as brothers. The Black Muslims have had remarkable successes in

> You learned to stand up straight and do something for yourself. You learn to be a lady at all times – to keep your house clean – to teach your children good manners. There is not a girl ... who does not know how to cook and sew. The children are very respectful; they speak only when they are spoken to. There is no such thing as letting your children talk back to you the way some people believe.
> (Ernestine X, Black Muslim 1966, quoted in John R. Howard, *The Making of a Black Muslim*, Transaction Vol. 4 No. 2, 1966)

spreading education among adult illiterates and in converting former criminals and drug addicts to a devout and orderly way of life. Wallace D. Muhammad, who took over the leadership upon the death of his father in 1975, has permitted white people to join the movement, which has been re-named "The World Community of Al-Islam in the West".

See also *Prophets*.

Calendar

The Muslim calendar is based on the lunar cycle and a year consists therefore of 354 days. In terms of the solar calendar, it moves "backwards" about eleven days each year. The starting-point of the Muslim calendar is 16 July 622, when the Prophet left Mecca for Medina, to establish the first Muslim community. This event is known as the *hijra* (also spelt "*hegira*") and is variously translated as the "exodus", "migration", or "breaking of ties". 16 July 622 is, therefore, I Muharram A H (Anno Hijrae) and there are roughly 103 Muslim (lunar) years for every 100 Christian (solar) ones. To calculate conversions from one calendar to another, the following formulae can be used. (C = Common Era year; H = *Hijra* year.)

$$C = H + 622 - \frac{H}{33}$$

$$H = C - 622 + \frac{C - 622}{32}$$

Muslims do not accept the nomination AD (Anno Domini) because they regard Jesus (Isa) as a true prophet but not a divine "lord". For the Christian calendar they use the nomination CE, meaning Common Era or Christian Era.

Because the Muslim calendar "moves" through the solar-based year, it bears no fixed relation to the seasons. Because the phases of the calendar depend upon the actual sighting of the moon, which can be obscured by cloud, precision is often difficult to obtain. A further source of possible confusion occurs from the fact that the Christian day is reckoned from midnight, whereas the Muslim day begins at sunset, conventionally reckoned at 6.00 pm.

See also *Astronomy, Fasting, Festivals, Hijra*.

The lunar year has 12 months, each of which begins after 29 or 30 days . . . when the crescent appears in the evening sky. As there is a total of only 354 days for these 12 months (more exactly 354.367) and the cycle of the seasons, which depends on the sun's movement, only recurs every 365 days (more exactly 365.242) the lunar year is approximately eleven days shorter than the solar year. In order to meet agricultural needs, a system of intercalation was needed . . . whereby an additional month was added, sometimes after 3 years, and other times after two. . . . The luni-solar calendar was used in Arabia until the end of the life of the Prophet, and it was only 3 months before his death that he gave the order to abolish it and to follow an absolute lunar calendar, without inter-calations. . . . The abolition of the luni-solar calendar simplified calculations, as a result of which the calendar could be understood by everyone. This was particularly important as it facilitated the religious practices of fasting and making the pilgrimage. With the absolute lunar calendar, Ramadan, the month of fast, could fall, by turns, in every season of the year. . . . If fasting were prescribed for a certain month of the solar calendar . . . its purpose would be vitiated by nature, for there is a six-month difference in seasons between the countries located in each of the two hemispheres. With the Islamic reform, fasting could be observed, alternately, in every season.
(Muhammad Hamidullah, "Muhammad, Prophet of God", *Cultures* Vol. VII No. 4, 1980, The Unesco Press and la Bacconière)

Caliphate

Muhammad's sudden death in 632 faced the Muslim community with a crisis of leadership. The crisis was resolved by the decision to recognize Abu Bakr, the Prophet's father-in-law and one of the earliest converts to Islam, as his *khalifa* – "successor". It was made very clear, however, that he was a successor to Muhammad's position only as a political leader and not as a prophet.

Caliphs claimed only to be defenders of the faith, not its expounders. And over the centuries the caliphate declined from being an effective political office to a purely symbolic one. Abu Bakr died after two years and was succeeded by Umar, who adopted the title "Commander of the Faithful", which remained thereafter the unique title of the Caliph. After Umar came Uthman and Ali, who moved the capital from Medina to Kufa in Iraq. These first four Caliphs all knew Muhammad closely and are known as the *rashidun* or "rightly guided" Caliphs. The period of their rule (632-61) is looked back on in Muslim tradition as a sort of golden age.

Ali's death was followed by the emergence of the Umayyad dynasty, who transferred the capital of the expanding Arab empire to Damascus, the chief city of the conquered Byzantine province of Syria. The Umayyad court was cultured, pleasure-loving and not particularly religious. Discontent in the empire led to the violent overthrow of the Umayyads in 750 (though one member of the family managed to escape to Spain, where he established a breakaway Umayyad caliphate). The succeeding dynasty, the Abbasids (who traced their descent from the Prophet's uncle, Abbas) shifted the seat of government again, to their purpose-built capital, Baghdad and restored something of the dignity and austerity of early Islam. But they remained lavish and enlightened patrons of learning and the arts. By the eleventh century, however, their effective power was on the wane. A rival Shi'ite caliphate had long been established in North Africa by the Fatimid dynasty (909-1171) and the Abbasids themselves were more or less puppets of their generals and courtiers.

The Abbasid dynasty was finally destroyed by the Mongols who sacked Baghdad in 1258 and the title of Caliph was taken over by the rulers of Egypt, a dynasty of Turkish slave-soldiers known as the Mamluks. When they in turn fell victim to

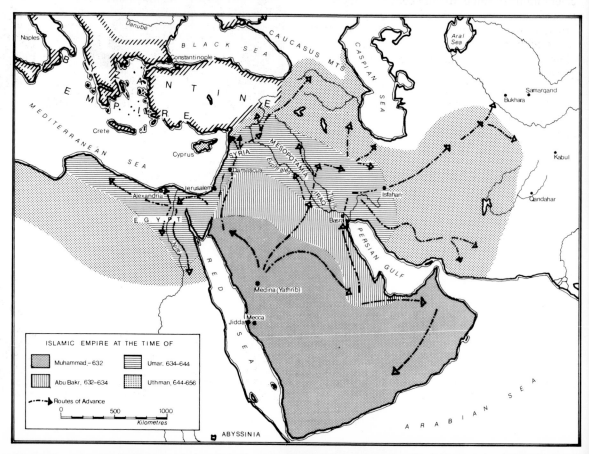

ISLAMIC EMPIRE AT THE TIME OF

Muhammad,–632

Umar, 634–644

Abu Bakr, 632–634

Uthman, 644-656

Routes of Advance

0   500   1000

Kilometres

the expanding Ottoman empire in 1517, the title passed to the Ottomans. It brought them perhaps some prestige, particularly in the more distant parts of the Islamic world, but it added little or nothing to their real power. The collapse of the Ottoman dynasty as a result of defeat in the First World War led to the final abolition of the caliphate when the Turkish Republic was proclaimed in 1924.

See also *Ali, Hijra, Muhammad, Politics, Shi'ites*.

Call to Prayer

See *Adhan*.

Calligraphy

See *Arabic Language, Architecture and Art, Bismillah, Shahada*.

Christianity

See *Black Muslims, Calendar, Dhimmi, Holy Men, Islam, Jerusalem, Jesus, Marriage, Mosques, Muslims in Britain*.

Circumcision

All Muslim males are circumcised, although this is not required by the Qur'an. The ceremony is invariably accompanied by feasting and celebration. In some Muslim communities the act is performed when the boy is still only a baby; in others it may be years later, but always before the onset of puberty. Circumcision, in the Muslim view, is strongly associated with ideas of personal cleanliness.

In some parts of the Muslim world, such as Arabia and the Sudan, female circumcision is practised, though without public ceremony. In recent times this custom has been severely criticized on psychological and medical grounds.

Special clothes, for the circumcision ceremony, on display in a shop window in Istanbul, Turkey.

Crescent

The crescent, which was probably taken over from ancient Persia as a symbol, appears quite early on as a decorative motif in Islamic art, but not until about the eighteenth century did it win general acceptance as a sign of Muslim identity. Nowadays it appears, often with a star, on the flags of many Muslim countries – for example, Malaysia, Pakistan and even Turkey, which is now a secular republic. The "Red Crescent" is the Muslim equivalent of the "Red Cross" disaster relief organization.

A crescent emblem surmounts symbols of Ottoman military prowess.

Death

See *Afterlife, Funerals.*

Dhimmi

Jews and Christians living under Muslim rule. Because Islam acknowledges Jews and Christians to be *ahl al-Kitab* ("People of the Book"), having a written revelation from God, they were allowed by the traditional Muslim empires such as the Ottomans to keep up their religions and were given the status of *dhimmi* ("protected persons"). As such, they were allowed to practise their own customs and forms of worship and to pass on their beliefs to their children. But they also had to wear distinctive clothes and pay an extra tax, had to seek permission to repair or extend their religious buildings, and were forbidden to bear arms or to try to convert others to their faith.

A Christian Jordanian family.

Divorce

For the Muslim, divorce is, in the words of the Prophet, the most hateful of all permitted things. Before Islam, men in Arabia were able simply to discard a wife whenever they wished. Islam introduced a compulsory interval (*idda*) of 3 months between a man's saying he wanted a divorce and the event's taking place, so that attempts at reconciliation could be made and it could be confirmed whether or not the wife was pregnant. If the wife was pregnant, the husband had to maintain her until the time of the birth. A divorced woman in Islam receives back the dowry (*mahr*) given to her upon marriage, as well as the contents of her household, but, after the divorce becomes final, her male relatives, rather than her former husband, must take on the responsibility for her upkeep, though he remains financially responsible for his children and may not always be given custody of them. Once a Muslim man has divorced his wife, he cannot re-marry her until she has married and divorced another man. The ritual of divorce is simple – a man announces three times (preferably on three separate occasions) his intention to divorce. But the simplicity of the procedure does not mean that Muslims turn to it easily. Family life is strong in Islam and many relatives will intervene to prevent marital problems reaching the point of divorce. Generally speaking, it is harder for a wife to divorce her husband than for a husband to divorce a wife.

See also *Law, Marriage, Women.*

. . . in view of the fact that human behaviour is changeable and sometimes unpredictable, Islam takes a realistic outlook on life and makes allowances for all unexpected events. . . . Islam does not accept or recognize any marriage which is not functional and effective. There can be no nominal or idle marriage. There must be successful marriage or no marriage at all. Marriage is too solemn a contract to be stationary or non-effective. So if it does not serve its purpose or function properly, it may be terminated. . . . But before taking this final and desperate step . . . the two parties involved must try to settle their disputes and solve their problems between themselves. If they fail two arbitrators, one from the husband's relations, the other from the wife's, must be commissioned to try to make peace between them and settle their differences. . . . Islam declares its policy that it cannot tolerate unhappy, cold and stagnant marriages which are much more harmful than divorce. . . . It does not force a person to suffer the injustice and harm of an unfaithful partner. It does not drive people to immorality. . . . It tells them this: either you live together legally and happily or else you separate in a dignified and decent way.
(Hammudah Abdalati, *Islam in Focus*, American Trust Publications, 1975)

Dress

Muslims, men as well as women, are enjoined by the Qur'an to dress modestly. This command has been variously interpreted in different Muslim countries and at different times in history. For many centuries, the practice of veiling was common among women, although it is not mentioned in the Qur'an; and some scholars argue that it is, in fact, a custom taken up from Persia after the conquest of that country. Nowadays, the veil is seen most often in Saudi Arabia and the Gulf countries. In Iran, the all-enveloping *chador* became a symbol of support for the "Islamic revolution" (1979) against the Shah, as in Algeria the veil had been the symbol of revolt against French colonial rule in the 1950s. In Egypt and Malaysia, Muslim traditionalists have also encouraged a revival of the veil and opposed the trend to western dress. Elsewhere, the veil is less common in big cities and small villages than in

O Prophet, say to thy wives and daughters and the believing women, that they draw their veils close to them; so it is likelier they will be known and not hurt. God is
All-forgiving, All-compassionate.

The Confederates (33:59)

Traditional Muslim dress in London's Hyde Park.

medium-sized towns, and less common among the wealthy, the young and the educated than among the poor and the old. Even among those who have given up the veil, however, it is often customary to keep the hair covered.

In Britain, Muslim standards of decency have sometimes been offended by school rules which require girls to wear skirts and blouses which leave legs and arms exposed. A workable compromise has been to allow Muslim girls to wear the traditional flowing *shalwar* (trousers) and *kameez* (tunic) in uniform cloth.

Muslim men are less obviously restricted in matters of dress but, like women, should avoid tight-fitting clothes, and, unlike women, are forbidden by some experts on Muslim law to wear gold, silk and the colour red.

Male pilgrims undertaking the *hajj* must wear only two unsewn sheets of white cloth. There is no special pilgrimage costume for women, but they must keep their faces unveiled.

See also *Purdah*.

Two styles of women's dress in modern Bahrain.

Economics

See *Waqf, Wealth, Zakat.*

Education

Islam has always stressed the importance of education. One of the most famous sayings attributed to the Prophet is "Look for knowledge, even if you have to go as far as China." Traditionally, education in Islam, at all levels, has focused on the Qur'an. Elementary education consisted of memorizing (though not necessarily understanding) long sections of the Qur'an and acquiring the rudiments of literacy and numeracy. Traditional Qur'an schools, with their emphasis on word-perfect rote-learning, still exist in many Muslim countries, alongside modern, western-style schools, and it is quite common for children to attend both. Higher education traditionally also focused on the Qur'an, which became the basis for studies of the Arabic language and Islamic law. *Madrasas* (colleges) giving certificates of attendance and qualification were established from the eleventh century onwards.

Muslim scholars made great advances in science, mathematics and medicine. At Baghdad the Caliph al-Mansur established the Bayt al-Hikmah (House of Wisdom), as a library and centre for translating learned works from foreign languages. But theological studies always out-ranked the sciences and humanities in prestige and it is al-Azhar, the bastion of religious orthodoxy, which has survived a thousand years and not the teaching-hospitals and astronomical observatories which were also once famous centres of scholarship.

Western-style education was introduced into many Muslim countries, on a limited scale, by western colonial powers such as Britain, France and the Netherlands. Independence has led to the spread of mass education, so that the majority of girls have been given effective access to education for the first time. Although Islam enjoined education upon men and women alike, and although early Islamic history provides numerous examples of learned women, the tendency in traditional Muslim societies was to provide education for boys far more than for girls, the great majority of whom remained illiterate. In Yemen, for instance, the first school for girls was opened as recently as 1964.

While the sciences are now well-established at university level in most Muslim countries, this does not mean that traditional learning is being

A traditional Qur'an class in north Africa.

displaced. In Malaysia, for example, courses in "Islamic Civilisation" have been introduced for all students, regardless of their own religion or main course of study. And in Egypt students have demanded separate teaching for men and women as is normal, for example, in Saudi Arabia.

The desire for education for their children was, for many Muslims, a major factor in their decision to emigrate to western countries. But Islamic religious beliefs and values do not always coincide with the customs and values of a typical western school. Most Muslim parents would prefer single-sex education, especially for teenage girls. Some object to their children receiving non-Islamic religious education. (They have the right in Britain to withdraw them from RE lessons and assembly.) Others dislike various aspects of the curriculum, such as art, PE, music, dancing and sex education. Uniform and food have also caused difficulties. Some schools have responded to the needs of their Muslim pupils by setting aside a place for prayer and making *halal* food available, but few have adapted their curriculum to enable Muslims to preserve their distinctive heritage and identity. For this reason, many supplementary schools have been established by mosques and Muslim educational organizations. Classes are usually held in the evenings or at week-ends. The emphasis is on teaching the Qur'an and the Arabic language, but some centres organize sports and recreations as well. Proposals to establish separate schools for Muslims, on the lines of Jewish and Catholic schools, have been discussed for many years, but only a few small-scale enterprises have been set up as yet.

See also *Arabic Language, al-Azhar, Dress, Hadith, Qur'an, Zakat.*

A Muslim school in the East End of London.

Preparing medicines, an illustration from a thirteenth-century manuscript. Note the bookstand by the seated figure.

Eid al-Adha, Eid al-Fitr

See *Festivals*.

Fasting

Muslims are encouraged to enjoy the good things of life, including food. But fasting (*saum*) once a year, throughout the twenty-nine days of the month of Ramadan, the ninth in the Muslim calendar, is also one of the "Pillars of the Faith". "O you who believe; Fasting is prescribed for you as it was prescribed for those before you that are expected to be truly obedient" (2:183). It was during Ramadan, on the "Night of Power", that the Qur'an was first revealed to Muhammad (sura 97) (2:185).

Fasting lasts from dawn (when a white thread can first be distinguished from a black thread) until dusk (when this is no longer possible) (2:187). In many Muslim cities it has been traditional to signal the beginning and end of the day's fast by firing a gun. Eating during the hours of darkness is permitted and many families have meals immediately after dusk and just before dawn.

Strictly speaking, the fast forbids the eating of food, the drinking of liquids (even swallowing one's own spittle), as well as smoking and any form of sexual contact. Because the Muslim, lunar calendar "moves" through the seasons, the hours of daylight, and therefore of fasting, are longer in some years than others. Going without liquids is probably harder in very hot climates than in more temperate ones. The month of fasting ends with the festival of *Eid al-Fitr*.

The very young, the very old, the sick and menstruating or pregnant women are exempt from the fast, as are travellers and soldiers on active service, though these last four categories should make up the days lost as soon as they are able to do so (2:184).

Fasting during Ramadan should also be accompanied by prayer, charitable gifts to the poor, contemplation and a complete reading of the Qur'an. Fasting is held to bring many benefits such as an increased awareness of the plight of the poor, greater self-discipline and a nearness to the condition of the angels.

Many Muslims who fail to perform their five daily prayers still make the effort to keep the fast of Ramadan. Voluntary fasts may also be observed at other times of the year but should not last more than three days at most. Many *sufis* have made it a rule to eat only every other day.

See also *Angels, Festivals, Zakat*.

> . . . one derives from fasting temporal advantages connected with hygiene, military training, development of will power . . . even as those resulting from the services of worship. . . . But it must be repeated that the aim is, essentially and chiefly a religious practice and a spiritual exercise enabling proximity to God. If one fasts for temporal motives only – under the prescription of a doctor for instance – he will be far from accomplishing his religious duty and will not benefit spiritually at all. . . . It may be recalled that the Prophet forbade fasts extending over several days continually (for 48 hours or 72 hours for instance) . . . even to those who longed to do so in their zeal for spiritual practices to obtain increased benefit. He remarked 'Thou hast obligations even with regard to thine own self.'. . . . In order to subjugate the body to the spirit it is necessary to break the force of the body and increase that of the spirit. It has been found that nothing is as efficacious for this purpose as hunger, thirst, renunciation of carnal desires and control of the tongue. . . . One of the aspects of individual perfection is the subordination of animal nature to reason and spirit.
> (Muhammad Hamidullah, *Introduction to Islam*, MWH London Publishers, 1979)

al-Fatiha

"The Opening", the first *sura* of the Qur'an and an essential element in all daily prayers. The two versions following show how difficult it is to reach an agreed translation of the Qur'an:

> In the Name of God, Most Gracious, Most
>   Merciful.
> Praise be to God,
> The Cherisher and Sustainer of the Worlds;
> Most Gracious, Most Merciful;
> Master of the Day of Judgment.
> Thee do we worship,
> And Thine aid we seek.
> Show us the straight way,
> The way of those on whom
> Thou hast bestowed Thy Grace,
> Those whose (portion)
> Is not wrath,
> And who go not astray.
> (Translation of Maulana Abul Kalam Azad, edited by Syed Abdul-Latif, Asia Publishing House, Bombay, 1962)

> In the name of Allah, the most Merciful, the
>   most Kind.
> All praise is for Allah, the Lord of the Universe,
>   the most Merciful, the most Kind;
> Master of the day of judgment.
> You alone we worship, from You alone we seek
>   help.
> Guide us along the straight path –
> the path of those whom You favoured, not of
>   those who deserve Your anger or went astray.
> (Ghulam Sarwar, *Islam: Beliefs and Teachings*, Muslim Educational Trust, 1982)
>   See also *Beliefs*, *Prayer*.

The Fatihah is a reminder to every leader and responsible man. . . . First you pray to God Who is merciful and compassionate. The next phrase is Lord of the *world* – not just the Arabs or the Muslims but the whole world. Then comes 'Owner of the Day of Judgement'. This is a reminder – to every statesman, every responsible person, every individual – of the fact that he will be responsible for what he does. It means that God knows what you try to hide. This consciousness of God's knowledge of events has a great effect. It gives a man courage and self control in his actions, in his words and even in his thinking. It gives him a guidance from within.
(Abderrahman al-Bazzaz, former Prime Minister of Iraq, quoted in Charis Waddy, *The Muslim Mind*, Longman, 1968)

It consists of seven verses, three concerning God, three man and one the relation between the two. In reciting its verses man stands in his primordial state before God, and prays in the name of all creatures and for all creatures. That is why its verbs are all in the first person plural and not the singular. It is the prayer of Man as the conscious centre of all creation before the Creator and as such it contains symbolically the total message of the Qur'an.
(Seyyed Hossein Nasr, *Ideals and Realities of Islam*, Allen and Unwin, 1966)

Fatimids

See *Caliphate*, *Shi'ites*.

Festivals

Festivals do not figure as prominently in Islam as in the world's other great religious traditions. In part, this may reflect the uncompromising monotheism of the Prophet Muhammad and his early Muslim companions, who were so concerned to stamp out pagan practices. In part, it may also reflect the fact that the requirement to perform five daily prayers and to follow the example of the Prophet in matters of dress, diet and personal hygiene generates such a sense of involvement and collective solidarity among believers that, when compared with other religions less demanding in these respects, Islam perhaps finds festivals almost unnecessary.

While this might be true in a Muslim country, where the everyday patterns of life in home, school, office or market-place bear the distinctive imprint of religious custom, Muslims in a non-Muslim country are likely to feel isolated. They welcome the opportunity that festivals bring to meet old friends and distant relatives and to re-affirm their membership of a world-wide community of believers.

It is certainly noteworthy that neither of the two main "official" festivals in Islam is mentioned in the Qur'an and that the extra prayers associated with them are regarded in religious law as desirable but not obligatory.

It is, however, also noteworthy that, whatever view Muslim theologians and intellectuals might have taken, among ordinary Muslims there has been a tendency both to enrich the approved festivals with folk observances and to add to their number either by incorporating pre-Islamic celebrations, such as the Persian New Year and the ancient Egyptian spring festival, or by developing new ones in relation to the memory of local holy men. This tendency has been so strong that the commemoration of the birthday of the Prophet (which probably began only in the thirteenth century) almost bids fair to rival the two *Eids* as a major festival in many parts of the Muslim world.

The two main festivals of Islam, *Eid al-Adha* and *Eid al-Fitr*, mark respectively the climax of the *Hajj* (the annual pilgrimage to Mecca) and the ending of the fast of Ramadan. Both of the *Eids* are celebrated with extra prayers, a sermon, mutual visiting by friends and relatives, a lavish meal and, especially for children, the giving of presents and the wearing of new clothes.

At *Eid al-Fitr* (end of Ramadan), believers should make a special charitable gift, *zakat al-Fitr*, which goes to the poor. At *Eid al-Adha* (Feast of Sacrifice) a third of the sacrifice should be given to the poor, the rest being consumed at a family feast. The act of sacrifice is performed by Muslims undertaking the *Hajj* and by fellow-believers throughout the world, who thus share in their experience.

See also *Circumcision, Hajj, Holy Men, Khutba, Marriage.*

At Eid so many people come to the mosque that it is necessary to prepare extra places outside for prayer.

Slaughtering an animal for Eid al-Adha in Pakistan.

Folk Religion

Alongside the orthodox religion of the Qur'an and *hadith*, there have grown up over the centuries many customs and beliefs which have little or no root in the Prophet's example and teachings. Sometimes these can be traced back to pagan practices existing in an area before the coming of Islam, sometimes to the influence of a neighbouring religious tradition such as Hinduism or Buddhism. Others appear to arise simply out of ignorance of what orthodox teaching is. In villages and in rural areas beyond the effective reach of mosques and *madrasas*, folk religion is more likely to flourish than in the great cities. The term "folk religion" covers a wide range of phenomena, from customs associated with rites of passage (birth, marriage and death) and the fortunes of the harvest, to belief in the power of the "evil eye", the use of the Qur'an as a protective talisman and the cult of spirit-possession. Folk religious practices have often been the target of criticism by religious reformers.

See also *Africa, Afterlife, Festivals, Holy Men, Islam in South East Asia.*

Food and Drink

A family meal in Baghdad, Iraq.

Muslims may eat only meat which has been slaughtered in the approved manner. This involves cutting through the animal's windpipe and carotid arteries while reciting the *bismillah* and thus acknowledging God as the creator of all living things and man's obligation not to take life thoughtlessly. After an animal has been slaughtered in this way, the blood must be drained away through the incision that has killed it. Only then is it *halal* (permitted). (Muslims may also eat Jewish *kosher* meat, which is slaughtered in a similar way.) Muslims may not eat meat which has been killed by other methods (for example, stunning) or which has died of disease or been sacrificed in the name of any other god (2:167). Carnivorous animals and birds are also forbidden, as is the domestic ass and the pig in any form (i.e. pork, ham, bacon and foods either containing or prepared in pig fat, such as some kinds of biscuit or ice cream). Margarines made from vegetable oils are permitted.

Alcoholic drinks are forbidden to Muslims (5:90-91) and some commentators on the Qur'an have extended the ban to stimulant drugs and even tobacco, though these have been generally consumed in many parts of the Muslim world, such as Yemen and Morocco. Alcohol should not be used in cooking or for medical purposes, unless there is positively no substitute. (The preservation of life must come first. Faced with starvation, a Muslim may eat foods which would otherwise be *haram* – forbidden.) A Muslim should not offer alcohol to a non-Muslim, nor sell it if he owns a shop or a restaurant. Muslims believe that alcohol not only leads to addiction and waste but also, because it diminishes a man's control over his mind, damages his ability to relate to God through prayer.

Muslims invariably eat only with the right hand, using the left hand only for toilet purposes. Hands should be washed and a grace said both before and after a meal.

See also *Fasting, Wahhabis*.

Funerals

In most Muslim countries death is immediately followed by the ritual wailing of the female relatives of the deceased. The corpse is then washed, clothed in a shroud and carried on a bier, sometimes to a mosque, but often straight to the cemetery. It is regarded as a good deed to accompany a funeral procession and men take turns to carry the body. Burial should take place within twenty-four hours. (In non-Muslim countries this requirement may cause difficulty with official regulations.) Cremation is not allowed for Muslims. The grave should be dug so that the corpse can be laid facing towards Mecca. Although elaborate tombs have often been built by Muslim rulers (for example, the Mughals) and to honour famous *sufi shaikhs*, they are frowned upon by some Muslims (for example, *Wahhabis*). At the graveside an *imam* usually leads the mourners in prayer, praising God and the Prophet. This is followed by silent prayer and the burial of the corpse. The *Fatiha* is then recited. Other funeral customs include giving food to the poor and reciting the Qur'an for several nights at the home of the bereaved. Mourning is usually brief and many *hadith* condemn excessive grief as an impious protest against God's will.

See also *Afterlife*.

A funeral procession in Tangier, Morocco.

al-Ghazzali

Philosopher and mystic, Abu Hamid al-Ghazzali (1058-1111) reconciled sufism with orthodoxy, both in his life and in his writings. Born in north-eastern Persia, he travelled to Iraq, where he showed himself to be a precociously able student and then a charismatic teacher, achieving the status of professor at thirty-three, which was half the age of most professors. Five years later he suddenly abandoned his brilliant academic career and went to live, quite literally, in the wilderness. Living in absolute poverty, meditating and practising ascetic exercises, he yet found time to write a spiritual autobiography, *The Deliverer from Error*. Returning at last to a conventional religious and social life, he summarized his philosophic outlook in a classic treatise, *The Reviving of the Religious Sciences*.

See also *Sufism*.

God

See *Allah*.

Hadith

Because Muslims regard Muhammad as both the "Messenger of God" and the perfect man, everything he said or did is important for them as a guide to living. During his lifetime many came to ask his advice on all sorts of everyday matters. Others simply tried to imitate even his smallest actions. The sayings and doings of the Prophet were recorded in great detail, first of all by people who had known him personally and then by people who had known these "companions" and later by people who knew people who knew . . . and so on back to the Prophet himself. The recorded sayings and doings of the Prophet are known as *hadith* (plural: *ahadith* – although, in English we use "*hadith*" as both singular and plural). The Arabic word is usually translated into English as "tradition", but the more literal meaning is "speech" or "news". Each *hadith* consists of the report (*matn* – text) of an incident or opinion, together with the line of witnesses (*isnad*) who transmitted it from the time of the Prophet.

During the two centuries after Muhammad's death, when Islam was expanding rapidly and Muslim rulers and the officials and scholars who served them were facing many new situations in which they had to judge whether the customs of conquered peoples were right or wrong, *hadith* supplied invaluable information to fill out the general guidelines laid down in the Qur'an. Because *hadith* gave rulers the authority to approve or forbid different customs, it became tempting to make up *hadith*, complete with a false chain of transmitters to "prove" their value. Muslim scholars therefore came to devote much effort to distinguishing between *hadith* that were "sound" (i.e. the best), "good" (the next best) and "doubtful", relying chiefly on their assessments of the character of the transmitters as the method for classifying them. Bukhari, the most celebrated of these scholars, is said to have examined more than half a million different examples of *hadith* (many of which were similar but claimed to come through different *isnad*); of these he accepted about 4,000 as sound. *Hadith* provide the most important source of Islamic law after the Qur'an itself.

See also *Jihad, Muhammad, Sunna*.

Hajj

Hajj is the name given to the pilgrimage to Mecca which is a duty for each Muslim once in his lifetime, provided he can afford to undertake the journey and does not endanger either his health or his family by doing so. The *hajj* is performed during the second week of the twelfth month of the Islamic calendar, *Dhull-Hijja*.

The main stages of the *hajj* are as follows:

(A) the pilgrim puts on *ihram* – gets into a state of ritual purity by putting on two white sheets of seamless cloth. This symbolizes purity, renunciation and the equality of believers, whose rank can no longer be distinguished by their dress. There is no prescribed dress for women, but they must go unveiled.

(B) the pilgrim enters the *haram*, the sacred area around Mecca, forbidden to non-Muslims, within which living things are protected from violence.

(C) the pilgrim enters the Great Mosque and walks seven times around the *Ka'ba*, the lifelong focus of his prayers, which Muslims regard as the oldest existing shrine for the worship of the one true God. The *Ka'ba* is believed to be the place where heavenly bliss and power touch the earth directly. According to Muslim tradition, it was built by Abraham.

(D) the pilgrim performs the *sa'y* – running seven times between the hills of Safa and Marwah, and so re-enacting the search of Hagar, servant of Abraham, for water for her infant son, Ishmael, from whom the Arabs hold themselves to be descended. This ritual expresses respect for maternal love, and gratitude to God, who made the sacred spring of Zamzam appear for Hagar's and Ishmael's relief.

(E) the pilgrim journeys to Mina, eight kilometres east of Mecca, to spend the night in prayer and meditation.

(F) the pilgrim goes to the plain of Arafat, where Muhammad preached his last sermon, to perform the rite of standing – supreme experience of the *hajj*. Starting when the sun passes the meridian, the pilgrims, while standing, pray and meditate

Hajj – stoning the devil at Mina.

until just before sunset. (Muslims believe that Adam and Eve, separated after their fall from Paradise, were re-united at Arafat, by God's grace.)

(G) after spending the night at Muzdalifah, the pilgrim proceeds to Mina just before daybreak and spends three nights there. During this time, on each of the three days, the pilgrim throws seven stones at each of three pillars (symbolic of devils who tempted Abraham not to sacrifice his son) and also sacrifices an animal, as a gesture of renunciation and thanksgiving, and in commemoration of the poor and of Abraham, who was willing to sacrifice his son, Ishmael. This sacrifice is also part of a world-wide celebration which unites Muslims everywhere in the common rite of *Eid al-Adha*.

Pilgrims interpret the *hajj* to themselves in a variety of ways – "a rehearsal for Resurrection Day" . . . "you go to please God, not yourself". Some have stressed the arduousness of the journey and the climate. But more frequently it is the intensity of the emotional experience which endures. Malcolm X, the American Black Muslim,

recorded in his autobiography: "They were of all colours, from blue-eyed blondes to black-skinned Africans. But we were all participating in the same ritual, displaying a spirit of unity and brotherhood that my experiences in America had led me to believe never could exist between the white and the non-white."

The organization of the *hajj* is an immense administrative task for the Saudi authorities; food, shelter, transport, interpreting and the prevention of disease are only a few of the major problems. Congestion is another: 120 planes a day arrive at Jeddah; almost two million pilgrims must be accommodated in a valley less than two kilometres wide, and the capacity of the Great Mosque is only 75,000. Modern technology has, therefore, been pressed to the service of ancient ritual and the Saudi government allocates some $280 million a year to the Ministry of Pilgrimage and Religious Endowment, to enable it to cope with organizing the *hajj* and to subsidize pilgrims' outlays on food, travel and accommodation.

See also *Abraham, Festivals, Islam in South East Asia, Ka'ba, Mecca.*

Heaven and Hell

See *Afterlife*.

Hijra

The *hijra* (often spelt *hegira*) was a central event in the early history of Islam, marking the decisive break between Muhammad's first period of preaching and persecution in his native Mecca and the establishment of the first community of Muslims, under his guidance, at Medina. Dated in 622 in the western calendar, the *hijra* also marks the start of the Muslim calendar.

The term *hijra* is often translated in English as "flight", but it would be more accurate to say "exodus", "emigration", or "the breaking of ties". It was brought about by the death of Muhammad's protector, his uncle Abu Talib, and the invitation from leading inhabitants of Yathrib (later named Madinat al-Nabi – the city of the Prophet) to come to live among them, settling their disputes and enjoying their protection. Muhammad first commanded his followers to leave Mecca as quietly as possible, singly or in small groups; then he

finally left himself, with Abu Bakr, who was to become the first Caliph. Many stories are told about the miracles which protected them from their pursuers on this journey.

See also *Calendar, Medina, Muhammad.*

Holy Men

Although orthodox Islam stresses the close and direct relationship between God and the believer,

Tomb of a marabout in the oasis at Tozeur, on the edge of the Sahara.

there has long been a cult of holy men who bridge the gulf between the two which may be experienced by simple folk and especially the illiterate, who cannot read the Qur'an for themselves. Often referred to by western writers as "saints", these holy men are not, strictly speaking, like saints in the Christian sense, who, to be recognized as such, must be both dead and officially canonized after a long process of judicial enquiry. Holy men in Islam have often been recognized as such during their own lives and depend for that recognition, not on the religious authorities, but on the spontaneous devotion of ordinary believers, who credit them with possession of *baraka* – spiritual power.

Variously described as a *marabout* (member of a monastery), *wali* (friend or person near God) or *shaikh* (old man), the holy man has been especially influential in the rural areas of North Africa and South Asia, acting as a spiritual guide to the devout

and a settler of disputes between communities in the absence of effective courts or governments. Some became the founders of major *sufi* orders, and *sufi* thinking has constructed an elaborate hierarchy of saints, whose existence is held to be vital for the spiritual well-being of the world.

The tomb of a holy man has frequently become a place of prayer (especially against illness and infertility) and also of pilgrimage, especially on the anniversary of his death. This date may become the occasion of a festival (in Arabic, *maulid;* in Turkish, *mevlid*), despite the disapproval of the orthodox. Many believers hope for the intercession of a holy man on the day of judgment, although this, too, is at variance with orthodox teaching.

See also *Folk Religion, Islam in South Asia, Sufism.*

Ibn Sina

Known to the west as Avicenna, Ibn Sina (980-1037) was a true polymath, whose expertise ranged from the abstractions of philosophy and the speculations of astronomy to the very real problems of statecraft and practical medicine. Born near Bukhara, he is said by the age of eighteen to have taught himself all the then-known

sciences and to have written an encyclopaedia of science by the time he was twenty-one. Over a hundred of his written works survive and his *Qanun,* a medical encyclopaedia, remained a standard textbook in both the Islamic world and the west for at least five centuries after his death.

Idolatry

Before the coming of Islam, the Arabs worshipped many different idols, in the form of sculptures and pictures. Tradition tells that more than three hundred were housed in the *Ka'ba*. Opposition to the worship of idols was a central and consistent aspect of Muhammad's teachings. Sura 25:3 emphasizes that idols can neither harm nor help. When Muhammad reconquered Mecca in 630, the *Ka'ba* was purged of its idols. As a result of Islam's hostility to idols, sculpture and painting have played only a minor part in the development of the arts of the Muslim world.

See also *Architecture and Art, Ka'ba.*

Imam

This is a word with two meanings, one general and one specific to Shi'a Islam. In general terms, an *imam* is the person who leads the prayers and preaches the Friday sermon in a mosque. Although the prayers may be led by any male Muslim of good character (a woman may lead the prayers if the congregation is entirely female), it has been usual, particularly in the larger mosques, for a trained *imam* to be employed. The *imam* is usually an expert on points of Islamic law and may also teach Arabic and the Qur'an as part of his duties. An *imam* is not, however, the same as a priest, for, in Islam, there are no sacraments and his participation is not, therefore, essential for the correct performance of such ceremonies as marriages and funerals.

In Shi'a Islam, the term *Imam* is used to describe the Prophet's son-in-law, Ali, and his descendants. Shi'a Muslims attribute great spiritual powers to these leaders of their community and do not acknowledge the authority of Caliphs, who were not in the line of hereditary succession from Ali. According to Shi'a Muslims, an *Imam* alone has the right and infallible ability to interpret Islam for the age in which he lives. Most Shi'ite Muslims belong to the Ithna 'Ashariyya (Twelver) school, which recognizes twelve *Imams*, from Ali to Muhammad al-Mahdi, who in 940 passed from earthly existence to rule, like his successors, through learned and pious men acting in his name. The other main branch of the Shi'a are the Isma'ilis or "Seveners" (*Sab'iyya*), who recognize seven *Imams* but are then further sub-divided, according to whom they recognize as their successors and representatives.

See also *Isma'ilis, Khutba, Prayer, Shi'ites.*

As used technically in Shi'ism the term refers to the person who contains within himself the 'Muhammadan Light' which was handed down through Fatimah, the daughter of the Blessed Prophet, and Ali, the first Imam, to the others, terminating with the Hidden Imam who is to appear again one day as the Mahdi. As a result of the presence of this light, the Imam is considered to be 'sinless' and to possess perfect knowledge. . . . The Imams are like a chain of light issuing forth from the 'Sun of Prophecy' which is their origin, and yet they are never separated from that Sun. Whatever is said by them emanates from the same inviolable treasury of inspired wisdom. Since they are an extension of the inner reality of the Blessed Prophet, their words really go back to him. That is why their sayings are seen in the Shi'ite perspective as an extension of the prophetic hadith, just as the light of their being is seen as a continuation of the prophetic light. . . . (Seyyed Hossein Nasr, Introduction to *A Shi'ite Anthology*, Muhammadi Trust, 1979)

Indonesia

See *Islam in South East Asia*.

Islam

> "This day I have perfected your religion for you, completed my favour upon you and have chosen for you Islam as your way of life" (5:3)

"Islam" is often translated as "submission", but a more accurate term would be "surrendering", because, through his worship of Allah and obedience to His Laws, the believer in Islam, the Muslim, makes active, conscious and continuous surrender of his will, rather than a once-and-for-all act of submission.

Islam is, after Christianity, the second most widely practised religion in the world, embracing at least one sixth of the human race. Muslims emphasize that Islam is more than a set of beliefs (*iman*) and acts of worship (*'ibadah*) (see *Pillars of the Faith*); it is a *din*, a complete way of life, combining creed and cult with manners and morals to produce a harmonious system for living. This explains the second meaning often given to the word *Islam* – "peace". By living according to Islam, Muslims believe that they will find peace with Allah, with each other and with the world around them.

Muslims believe that all people are born Muslims and that it is their parents who turn them from the "straight path" of Islam by bringing them up according to the dictates of another religion. In this connection, it is interesting to note that the Qur'an uses the term "Muslim" to refer not only to the followers of Muhammad but also to Abraham and the disciples of Jesus (for instance, 22:78: "He named you Muslims before and in this").

All that is required of a convert to Islam is that he or she should recite the profession of faith with complete sincerity before a believing Muslim.

See also *Allah, Beliefs, al-Fatiha, Jahiliya, Pillars of the Faith*.

Islam proclaims an order and pattern in the universe and exhorts the believer to conform to it.

Islam in South Asia

Muslim conquerors reached the north-western frontiers of India as early as the eighth century, but permanent conquest, as opposed to raiding, came some five centuries later, with the establishment of the Delhi sultanate. In the sixteenth century the Mughals, a dynasty descended from the Mongols, established a powerful empire centred on northern India and later extended their authority over the rest of the sub-continent. Political control did not, however, lead to mass conversions to the religion and the bulk of the population stayed faithful to Hinduism; the rise of Sikhism can also be seen as, to some extent, a reaction against Muslim influence.

Generous patrons of the arts, the Mughals dazzled European visitors with their magnificence but gradually lost their authority after the death of Aurangzeb (1618-1707), although the dynasty did not formally end until the great rebellion of 1857-8. Under British rule, which followed the decline of Mughal power, Muslims enjoyed a relatively privileged position. The prospect of independence, however, led to a general fear of domination by India's great Hindu majority and consequently to the demand for a separate state for Muslims – Pakistan ("Land of the Pure"). This was eventually achieved in 1947, despite the misgivings of the withdrawing British and of some leading Indian nationalists, and at the cost of considerable bloodshed as Muslims fled from areas where they were in the minority. Islam remains the religion of the overwhelming majority of the populations of Pakistan and Bangla-Desh (which was a part of Pakistan until 1971), but in India itself it is still a minority faith, like Christianity or Sikhism.

Islam in South Asia has long been marked by the influence of *sufi* mystics, who were active in spreading the faith throughout the region. Even today, many South Asian Muslims turn to a *pir* or holy man for spiritual guidance.

Famous South Asian Muslims include Sir Sayyid Ahmed Khan (1817-98), who believed that the teachings of Islam could be reconciled with the discoveries of modern science and founded a college which became the Muslim University of Aligarh; and Sir Muhammad Iqbal (c. 1875-1939), a celebrated poet in both English and Urdu, which has become the national language of the Pakistan for which he so ardently campaigned.

See also *Ahmadiyya, Sufism*.

A Mughal garden – vision of paradise.

Islam in South East Asia

Islam is the majority religion in Malaysia and in Indonesia, the latter being the country with the largest Muslim population in the world. Significant Muslim minorities are also found in Buddhist Thailand and Burma and the Christian Philippines. Islam came to the region by peaceful conversion by merchants rather than by armed conquest and was well-established by the sixteenth century. The strength of pre-existing religious traditions and the great distance between the region and the heartland of the orthodox faith in Arabia led to the persistence of folk-beliefs (e.g. in tree-spirits) and customs (e.g. eating pork) at variance with the strict teachings of the Qur'an and *sunna*. The coming of steamship travel after 1870 brought a great surge of participation in the *hajj* and consequent close contact with orthodox teaching. The result was a series of reform movements aiming to "purify" local Muslims of unorthodox customs. Islam continues to be a major factor in the politics, culture and social life of the region.

See also *Folk Religion, Hajj.*

Isma'ilis

Isma'ilis are a sub-group of Shi'ite Islam. Like other Shi'ites they hold that, after Muhammad's death, Ali succeeded to the spiritual leadership of the Muslim community and passed it on to his descendants. Unlike most Shi'ites, who acknowledge twelve Imams, the Isma'ilis recognize a continuous succession. They separated from other Shi'ites in giving allegiance to Isma'il, the chosen successor of the sixth Imam, Ja'far al Sadiq (d. 765). The greatest political success of the Isma'ilis was the creation in Egypt and Syria of the Fatimid caliphate (909-1171).

The Isma'ilis believe that the Qur'an has an inner meaning, accessible to believers only through the Imams. Isma'ili thinkers made outstanding contributions to Islamic philosophy, but differences about the succession split the movement into sub-groups, such as the Druzes, Bohoras and Nizaris (also known as Khojas) who form the largest group of Isma'ilis today. Widely-scattered throughout the world, in Britain they form a well-organized and prosperous community, who acknowledge the Aga Khan as the forty-ninth in the line of succession to the Imamate.

See also *Ali, al-Azhar, Imam, Shi'ites.*

The Isma'ili Centre, London.

Jahiliya

The "age of barbarism" before the coming of Islam. Pre-Islamic Arabia was characterized by polytheism (worship of many gods), idolatry (worship of images), human sacrifice and much social injustice, violence and disorder. Muhammad's teachings emphasized monotheism (worship of one god), prayer, charity and righteous living, thus constituting a moral as well as a religious revolution in his native land.

See also *Idolatry, Islam, Ka'ba.*

Jerusalem

Jerusalem is for Muslims the third most sacred city, after Mecca and Medina, and is called in Arabic *al-Quds*, "the holy". For a year or so after the *hijra* Muslims were enjoined to pray facing towards Jerusalem, until a later revelation ordered Muhammad to change the *qibla* to Mecca. Conquered by Arab armies in the reign of Umar (634-44), Jerusalem was venerated as the starting point of the Prophet's *miraj*, a miraculous night journey to heaven from the place where Solomon's temple once stood. In 691 the Caliph Abd al-Malik built the Dome of the Rock on this spot, which is also held by tradition to be the place where the angel Israfil will sound the call to judgment on the last day. The present building was largely restored by the Ottoman architect Sinan in the sixteenth century. Nearby, also on the Temple Mount, stands the ancient Aqsa mosque, which contains a *mihrab* given by Saladin, its rebuilder. It has been the target of politically motivated attacks in recent years. Access to, and control of, the holy places in Jerusalem remains a source of tension between

The first great monument of Islam – the Dome of the Rock, Jerusalem.

Israel, which occupies the city, and the governments of many Muslim countries, just as it was between Muslims and Christians at the time of the Crusaders, who controlled the city from 1099 to 1187.

See also *Qibla*.

38

Jesus

Jesus (in Arabic, Isa) is referred to no fewer than twenty-five times in the Qur'an, which mentions the Annunciation (3:37 and 19:16), the Virgin Birth (19:22) and various of his miracles (3:43 and 5:109). Muslims accept Jesus as a prophet, but do not regard him as the Son of God. Nor do they believe that he was crucified (4:156), holding that God substituted another in his place and raised him up to Himself. Islam's denial of the two central doctrines of Christianity – the Trinity and the Incarnation – shows the most profound difference in belief between the two religions. Muslims believe that to claim that God has a son or any other "associate" would be to be guilty of *shirk*, associating another being with God and thereby compromising His one-ness (*tawhid*). Later Muslim traditions often portrayed Jesus as a judge whose second coming would begin the end of the world. Other traditions stressed his rejection of worldly goods and pleasures.

See also *Allah, Calendar, Mahdi, Prophets.*

> *And when Jesus came with the clear signs he said, 'I have come to you with wisdom, and that I may make clear to you some of that whereon you are at variance: so fear you God and obey you me. Assuredly God is my Lord and your Lord; therefore serve Him; this is a straight path.'*
>
> *Ornaments (43:64)*

Jews

See *Dhimmi, Jerusalem, Marriage, Medina, Muslims in Britain.*

Jihad

Jihad, often translated simply as "holy war", means "striving" and is sometimes referred to as the "sixth pillar of Islam". Muslims, and especially *sufis*, often distinguish between the "lesser" *jihad*, bearing arms in defence of Islam, and the "greater" *jihad*, the constant struggle each Muslim should undertake to ensure that the spirit of Islam prevails both within himself and among those around him, by persuasion and example. According to a *hadith* reported by Bukhari, "the best *jihad* is to speak the truth before a tyrant ruler".

While many wars of conquest and ambition have been fought under the cloak of *jihad*, it should properly be proclaimed only when the practice of Islam is threatened by an unbelieving enemy, as during the early days of the conflict of Mecca against Medina (8:39;9:124). There are elaborate rules for the protection of non-combatants, such as women and children; and all those who fall "in the cause of Allah" are martyrs who will immediately pass into paradise (2:154; 3:169,195).

See also *Africa, Afterlife, Mosque.*

> It *may* require fighting in God's cause, as a form of self-sacrifice. But its essence consists in: (1) a true and sincere faith which so fixes its gaze on God, that all selfish and worldly motives seem paltry and fade away; and (2) an earnest and ceaseless activity, involving the sacrifice (if need be) of life, person or property, in the service of God. Mere brutal fighting is opposed to the whole spirit of Jihad, while the sincere scholar's pen or the preacher's voice or the wealthy man's contributions may be the most valuable form of Jihad.
> (Abdullah Yusuf Ali, *The Holy Qur'an: Text, Translation and Commentary*, Dar al Arabia, Beirut, 1965)

Jinn

Jinn (sometimes written *"djinn"* and anglicized as "genies") are neither men nor angels but beings created from fire who are mentioned frequently in the Qur'an, usually as tempters to evil or demons who take possession of the unwary. Muslim tradition holds that *jinn* are often found in lonely places and are usually invisible but can appear in human or other form. Some modern Muslim scholars have explained the Qur'anic references to *jinn* as a poetic expression of the natural forces of the universe, neither good nor evil in themselves, though often a cause of human tragedy.

Ka'ba

Often spelt *"Ka'aba"* and meaning literally "cube", this is the central shrine of Islam and the point towards which all Muslims turn when they pray (2:142). It stands at the centre of the Grand Mosque in Mecca and is the only place where believers pray in concentric circles rather than in straight rows. Muslim tradition holds that the *Ka'ba* was first built by Adam, then rebuilt by Abraham and restored again during the time of Muhammad, whose grandfather was once its official guardian. By Muhammad's time the *Ka'ba* had ceased to be a shrine to the one true god and was crowded with more than three hundred idols which the Prophet destroyed when he returned in triumph to Mecca in 630. The *Ka'ba* has remained, however, a central focus for the rites of pilgrimage, as it was in pre-Islamic times (3:90). Muslim tradition holds the *Ka'ba* to be the centre of the earth, the point at which God's creation began, lying directly below God's throne in heaven. It is one of the most powerful of all symbols in Islam and instantly recognizable to Muslims everywhere.

The *Ka'ba* is built of granite and is twelve metres long, ten metres wide and fifteen metres high. Set in the south-east corner, about one and a half metres above ground level, is a black stone which is said to have fallen from heaven and which pilgrims touch or kiss as a mark of reverence for the shrine as they walk around it. On the north-east wall is the *Ka'ba*'s only door; set two metres above the ground, it is reached by mobile steps which are used when the interior is washed with rose-water at the time of the *hajj*. The interior is empty except for gold and silver lamps hanging from the ceiling. The exterior is usually covered by a thick black cloth (*kiswa* – robe), embroidered in gold with verses from the Qur'an.

See also *Abraham, Hajj, Jahiliya, Mecca, Prayer.*

The Ka'ba, a tile picture from the wall of a Turkish mosque.

Khutba

The sermon given by a *khatib* (preacher), usually the *imam*, at the midday Friday service in the mosque and at the time of the two *Eids*. It precedes the congregational prayers and is delivered from a *minbar* (pulpit). Normally, it consists of two sections, the first being formal praises of God and the Prophet and recitation from the Qur'an and the second dealing, from a religious point of view, with a topic of current concern. In Britain the sermon is often given in both Arabic and English.

See also *Imam, Mosque.*

Khutba delivered in the Blue Mosque, Istanbul.

Koran

See *Qur'an.*

Law

Law in Islam is the expression not of Man's will but of God's. Because Muslims regard Islam as a "complete way of life", rather than simply a set of beliefs, a detailed code of behaviour has been evolved from the Qur'an and the *hadith* and, where these sources have proved lacking in detail, by analogy (*qiyas*) and through the consensus of opinion (*ijma'*) among those learned in the law who are known as the *'ulama*. This overall code of behaviour (*shari'a*) has been elaborated into four main schools of law (*fiqh*) which prevail in different parts of the Muslim world. Each was founded by a great jurist: Abu Hanifa (d. 767), Malik ibn Anas (d. 795), Al-Shafii (d. 820) and Ahmad ibn Hanbal (d. 855). (The Shi'ites have their own code of law, based on their own collections of *hadith*, although it is not vastly different from the others.) All the schools of law, while differing in details of procedure, arrange human actions into five categories: obligatory (*fard*), recommended (*mandub*), indifferent (*mubah*), disapproved (*makruh*) and forbidden (*haram*). In modern times, many Muslim countries have adopted various aspects of western law (for example, in respect of commerce or crime or constitutions), while maintaining shari'a law in personal and family matters such as divorce or inheritance.

See also *Hadith, Qur'an, 'Ulama.*

Madrasas

See *Education*.

Mahdi

Meaning literally "the guided one", this is a title bestowed by Muslims on leaders throughout history who have appeared as revivers of the faith in times of weakness and discontent. Muslim tradition also holds that the end of the world will begin when a *mahdi* (often identified with Jesus or a descendant of Muhammad) comes to establish a reign of justice on earth. In Shi'ite Islam the *mahdi* is identified with the Hidden *Imam* who disappeared in 878 and, it is predicted, will one day reappear and rule in God's name. The most celebrated example of a *mahdi* in recent history was Muhammad Ahmad (1844-85) who established an Islamic state in the Sudan which lasted from 1882 to 1898.

See also *Shi'ites*.

> If the expectation that Islam will eventually dominate the world . . . is genuine, then the coming of a great leader is also certain. People who look askance at the idea surprise me by their lack of common sense. When leaders of iniquity like Lenin and Hitler can appear on the stage of this world, why should the appearance of a Leader of Goodness only be regarded as remote and uncertain?
> (Abu al-Ala al-Mawdudi, "A Short History of the Revivalist Movement in Islam", quoted in John Alden Williams, *Themes of Islamic Civilization*, University of California Press, 1960)

Marriage

Muslims are encouraged to marry and a man may have up to four wives, though he must treat each of them the same. But having only one wife is recommended and, in practice, this has been the case for most Muslims throughout history. Only when a first wife is unable to bear children or has fallen seriously ill, is it usually thought advisable to take a second. And a Muslim wife may specify in her marriage contract that her husband must ask her permission before taking a second wife. Male Muslims may marry Jewish or Christian women but, otherwise, marriage outside the faith is forbidden.

The marriage ceremony involves the signing of a formal contract between the bridegroom and the bride's male guardian (usually her father or other close male relation) before two respected male Muslims. The contract usually specifies a sum of money (*mahr*) which comes from the husband's family and remains the wife's property in case of divorce. Festivities follow. In many Muslim countries, these often take the form of a ceremonial procession from the home of the bride's family to her new home. There is usually also an elaborate feast; although this is not formally required to make the marriage legally valid, it is usually thought to be a social necessity.

After marriage, women retain the separate ownership of any property they have had and have no duty to use it to support themselves or their

Posing for wedding photographs in Ankara, Turkey, where the civil ceremony is compulsory and the religious one optional.

children. This remains the responsibility of the husband. The wife's major responsibility is to provide a good home for her husband and children. She may work outside the home, providing this does not interfere with her major responsibility towards her family.

See also *Divorce, Women.*

Malaysian bride and groom praying at their wedding.

Mecca

Also spelt "Makka". Mecca is the birthplace of the Prophet Muhammad, the site of the *Ka'ba* and the sacred well Zamzam, the focus of prayer and pilgrimage and, therefore, the spiritual and psychological centre of the Muslim world. Even in pre-Islamic times it lay at the heart of a region of special sanctity – a place of worship, celebration and truce, free from violence. Now, with the territory around Medina, this region constitutes the *haramain* (*haram*=forbidden) which may only be entered by Muslims.

As a watering-place and sanctuary, Mecca attracted traders and pilgrims and, despite its inhospitable situation in a mountainous, infertile

> *From whatsoever place thou issuest, turn thy face towards the Holy Mosque; and wherever you may be, turn your faces towards it,*
>
> *The Cow (2:145)*

Mecca. Note the Ka'ba in the centre and the evident presence of the motor car in surrounding streets.

area, became a mercantile city of some importance in the sixth and seventh centuries of the Christian era, dominated by the tribe of Quraish and controlling the trade route from Yemen to Syria. The resulting wealth of both trade and pilgrimage brought about severe social problems, to which Muhammad's teaching appeared a decisive answer. His departure (*hijra*) from Mecca and subsequent triumphant return as both pilgrim and conqueror confirmed the city as a spiritual rather than a political centre. In recent years, large parts of the old quarters of the city have been demolished to make way for modern buildings and the motor car, but it remains the heart of Islam.

See also *Funerals, Hajj, Hijra, Ka'ba, Muhammad.*

Medina

Medina is short for Madinat al-Nabi – "the city of the Prophet". Originally called Yathrib, it was a settled oasis rather than a true city at the time of the *hijra*, when Muhammad and his followers migrated from Mecca. At Medina was founded the first ever community of Muslims living under the rule of Islam and here the Prophet, according to tradition, helped to build with his own hands the first mosque. Here he lies buried, as do Abu Bakr and Umar. Here Muhammad established the "Constitution of Medina", to regulate relations between the various Arab and Jewish tribes which inhabited the area, thus foreshadowing the principles of Islamic statecraft. After Muhammad's death Medina remained the capital of the empire until Ali removed it to Kufa in Iraq. But Medina remains the second most holy city of Islam and, like Mecca, is part of the *haramain*, accessible only to Muslims.

See also *Hijra, Mosque, Muhammad, Umma*.

Muhammad spent the last ten years of his life erecting the City of the Prophet, in its religious and social dimensions. Through these, the consequences of the hijra were to be multiple and lasting, establishing a model which the companions would transmit to future generations. . . . Muhammad was buried in situ and his tomb remained the symbol of the Prophet's City. . . . Every Moslem who visits the shrine feels in the presence of the Prophet and hears, as it were in his heart, the echo of his teaching.
(Emel Esin, "The Hijra and its Cultural Consequences", *Cultures* Vol. VII No. 4, 1980, The Unesco Press and la Bacconière)

Mihrab

See *Qibla*.

Minbar

See *Khutba*.

Miraj

See *Jerusalem*.

Mosque

A mosque (*masjid*) is literally "a place for prostration", but throughout the history of Islam it has been much more than a place of worship (see *Prayer*), serving as school, council chamber, law court and community centre. Traditionally, the local mosque also served as the starting point for the *hajj* and the place where *jihad* was proclaimed.

The very simplicity and bareness of the mosque have enhanced its versatility, for, apart from rugs and lamps, a pulpit (*minbar*) and a pool or fountain for washing, the mosque is usually empty of furnishings. Its beauty derives from the proportions of its construction and the harmony of its decoration, in tile, stucco or mosaic.

The first mosque was built with his own hands by the Prophet in Medina, and part of it doubled as his home. All subsequent mosques, however grand or complex, follow the same basic model,

Prayers in a mosque teach us brotherhood and equality of mankind as in a mosque we find people of all races and classes standing shoulder to shoulder without any discrimination of colour, rank, wealth or office. The king may find a labourer standing next to him, a private may be standing next to a general. No worshipper may object to another worshipper standing next to him. All are equal in the House of Allah.
(Rashid Ahmad Chaudhri, *Mosque: its importance in the life of a Muslim*, The London Mosque, 1982)

Shoes are removed on entering the mosque.

POLITENESS ALL VISITORS ARE REGUESTED TO RESPECT
THE RELIGIONS SANCTUARY
_WEARING CONSERVATIVE DRESS BY
_SPEAKING QUIETLY
_NOT SMOKING
_BEHAVING WITH DECORUM

HOURS
EVERY DAY 8ʰ AM to 12:30 PM
EXCEPT FRIDAY 8ʰ_ "_" noon
EVENINGS
JAN 3:30_ 5.30 Pm. JUNE 4_ 5.30. Pm
JULI 5_7 Pm . DEC 4'_ 7 Pm

Guidelines for tourist visitors in Tunisia.

Slim "pencil" minarets set off the vast hulk of this distinctive Ottoman mosque in Istanbul.

consisting of a covered hall for prayer and a walled courtyard (*sahn*) for assembly and ablution. The focal point of the mosque is the *mihrab*, a niche which denotes the direction of prayer. Although empty, it may be richly decorated. The mosque, unlike a Shinto shrine or Sikh *gurdwara*, is not considered to be God's special dwelling-place; nevertheless, shoes must not be worn within its precincts.

Most mosques have one or more minarets, towers from which the *muezzin* gives the *adhan*. In some areas minarets have been used as watch-towers or served as land lighthouses to guide travellers.

In the early days of Islam, when the Arab empire was expanding very rapidly, many churches were converted into mosques. Nowadays, in Britain and other countries where Christians are the most numerous religious group, Muslims are buying disused churches and converting them for the purposes of worship, education and community life.

See also *Adhan, Architecture and Art, Education, Muslims in Britain, Qibla, Waqf.*

Muezzin

A person who makes the call to prayer (*adhan*). This can be done by any adult male Muslim of good character, but professional *muezzins* have been usual. Quite often they were blind people. One reason for this was that it was an honourable occupation for someone who might otherwise have had difficulty finding work. Another was that a blind person, standing high up in a minaret (see *Mosque*), would not be able to look down into the private courtyards of houses.

See also *Adhan*.

Muezzin, Pakistan.

Mughals

See *Islam in South Asia*.

Muhammad

Muslims often claim that more is known about the life and personality of the Prophet than about the central figure of any of the other major religious traditions. Some western scholars are more sceptical, arguing that Muslim sources for the Prophet's biography date from no earlier than the early eighth century. Muhammad was born around 570 CE.

In a tribally-organized society like pre-Islamic Arabia, social standing depended largely on birth. It is therefore significant that Muhammad was born into the noble tribe of Quraish and that his grandfather was the guardian of the *Ka'ba*, the central shrine of Mecca, the Prophet's birthplace.

Muslim tradition has made much of the portents which are alleged to have accompanied the birth of the Prophet, though many of these "signs" have been discounted by the orthodox. Nevertheless, stories and tales of miraculous doings by the Prophet during his childhood have long been part of Muslim tradition.

Muhammad was born after the death of his father, and his mother died when he was two, leaving him to be brought up under the protection first of his grandfather and then of his uncle, Abu Talib. The Qur'an contains many references to the plight of orphans.

As he grew up, Muhammad found work with the merchant caravans of his native city, travelled far afield and won the name "*al-amin*", "the trustworthy". At the age of twenty-five, he

Never before or since has a prophet won such success so quickly; nor has the work of a single man so rapidly and radically transformed the course of world history. Through his inspired utterances, his personal example and the organizational framework he established for Islam, Muhammad laid the basis for a distinctive new style of life, which within the space of two centuries attracted the allegiance of a major fraction of the human race . . .
(W.H. McNeill, *The Rise of the West: A History of the Human Community*, University of Chicago Press, 1963)

Muhammad's life is the shining example for us to follow. He left for us teachings for all areas . . . of our life. His life is the complete embodiment of Islam. . . . Muhammad was raised for mankind, to show them the best way to worship Allah . . .
(Ghulam Sarwar, *Islam: Beliefs and Teachings*, Muslim Educational Trust, 1980)

married his employer, Khadija, a wealthy widow. Until her death he took no other wife. Sura 93:6-8 neatly summarizes the Prophet's career to that point: "Did he not find you as an orphan and give you a home, and find you in error and rightly guide you, and find you impoverished and make you rich?"

Muhammad, having risen out of poverty and established a reputation for shrewdness, certainly had the opportunity to become one of the rich merchants who controlled Mecca. Instead, he chose to devote himself to meditation, trying to work out why the people of Mecca treated each other so badly and worshipped false gods.

Revelation came for the first time in 610, as a terrifying experience in a cave on Mount Hira. The Prophet thought he was possessed by a devil. His wife reassured him and the experience was repeated over succeeding months. But not until 613 did he begin to declare his revelations openly.

Muhammad's (or rather, from the Muslim point of view, God's) message was concerned to stress the oneness of God, the duty of man to worship Him and live in accordance with His commands, and the reality of an afterlife in which each soul would be held accountable for its earthly actions and judged accordingly. These teachings were greeted with contempt by many Meccans. When Muhammad began to attack their misuse of power and wealth, and the false claims of idol-worshippers, contempt turned to hostility. Sheltered by the protection of his clan (by no means all of whom accepted his claim to prophethood), Muhammad was able to continue and gain converts, chiefly among the younger and poorer members of the community.

The year 619 brought a double blow – the deaths of Khadija and of Muhammad's uncle. The Prophet lost both his companion and his protector. Isolated and vulnerable, he sought a refuge for his followers and eventually found it in the oasis settlement of Yathrib, to which he was invited by local clan leaders anxious to gain a man of reputation who could settle the various disputes which upset their community. Yathrib later became known as Madinat al-Nabi ("the city of the Prophet") or, more simply, Medina.

Muhammad's departure (*hijra*) from Mecca to Medina in 622 was a turning-point both in the biography of the Prophet and in the history of Islam. It marked the establishment of the first Muslim community and the beginning of the Islamic calendar.

The story of Muhammad's stay in Medina is a complex one. His personal authority grew and this was accompanied by the elaboration, through continued revelation, of an increasingly comprehensive code of beliefs and behaviour for Muslims. At the same time, there were campaigns of armed struggle against both local resistance to these developments and Meccan attempts to crush the small but growing Muslim community.

Muhammad eventually overcame all challenges to his mission and lived to return to his native city, in an almost bloodless triumph, in 630. He purged it of idolatry and received acknowledgements of his authority from the tribes of most of the rest of the vast Arabian peninsula. By the time of his sudden death in 632, Islam was established and expanding, not merely as a faith but as a state and, increasingly, as a civilization.

See also *Caliphate, Festivals, Hadith, Jahiliya, Jerusalem, Mecca, Medina, Prophets, Qur'an, Sunna.*

Muslim Brethren

The *Ikhwan al-Muslimun*, also translated as "the Muslim Brotherhood", is a movement established in Egypt in 1927 by a former school-teacher, Hasan al-Banna (1906-49). Modelled to some extent on contemporary fascist movements, with a strong emphasis on organization, discipline and devotion to the leader, it sought to use the methods of the west to combat the spread of western values and customs in what was a deeply-conservative but rapidly-changing society. It combined a militant defence of tradition with a proclaimed concern to improve economic conditions and restore social justice. Its provision of health, education and welfare programmes won the organization widespread support, especially among the poorer classes in urban areas. At the peak of its power, in the late 1940s, it may have had as many as half a million members or even more. It had spread beyond Egypt into Syria, Iraq, Jordan, Palestine and the Sudan and was sending guerilla fighters to harass both Israeli and British troops in the region. The assassination of the founder and differences with the Free Officers movement, which came to power in Egypt in 1952, led to the official suppression of the movement. However, it continued many of its activities underground. Successively banned and tolerated by the authorities in different countries ever since that time, the organization remains a political and social factor whose strength cannot be precisely calculated but should not be ignored.

Muslims in Britain

The Muslim community in Britain dates back certainly to the early nineteenth century, when sailors from India and Yemen began to settle in riverside areas such as London and South Shields. The first mosque in England, which is still standing, was opened at Woking, Surrey in 1889. Most Muslims in Britain, however, have arrived since the partition of India in 1947, some as refugees (for example, from Kashmir and the Punjab in 1947-8, from East Africa in the early 1970s and from Lebanon in the later 1970s) but most of them attracted by the economic and educational opportunities open to them in their adopted country. In the 1950s and early 1960s the Muslim community consisted largely of single adult males, but since then, families have been re-united and a more balanced and settled community has resulted, although the proportion of older people is still markedly smaller than in British society as a whole or than it would be in the countries from which the migrants have come.

As far as countries of origin are concerned, the most important are Pakistan, India, Bangla-Desh, Nigeria and Cyprus, with a sizeable but temporary population of students from Malaysia and various Middle Eastern countries. More and more Muslim children are, of course, British-born and there is also a small but significant minority within the community of British converts to the religion. Estimates of the number of Muslims in Britain vary widely, ranging from 500,000 to 2 million. One million is probably a fair guess – and this would make the Muslim community twice as large as the Jewish community and thus the largest non-Christian minority in the country. The distribution of Muslims tends to be biased towards large industrial conurbations such as London, the West Midlands, Merseyside and West Yorkshire.

The growth of a settled community has been accompanied by a programme of mosque-building and there are probably more than 500 now, in different parts of the country. Many of the smaller ones are simply converted houses and others are converted churches, but there are also splendid, purpose-built ones in such cities as London, Glasgow and Manchester. Mosques not only act as centres for worship but often organize a wide range of social, welfare and educational activities. These are also provided by institutions such as the Muslim Educational Trust (London) and the Islamic Foundation (Leicester), while bodies like the Islamic Council of Europe, the Islamic Cultural Centre and the Union of Muslim Organizations try

The first mosque in Britain, built in Woking, Surrey, a century ago.

Yusuf Islam, a famous convert to Islam, formerly the singer, Cat Stevens.

to speak on behalf of the community as a whole.

While, originally, many Muslims were employed in unskilled or semi-skilled manual work, they are increasingly represented now in a wide range of occupations, in business (particularly textiles and retailing) and the professions (particularly medicine).

Substantial Muslim communities also exist in France (mostly from North Africa), West Germany (mostly from Turkey) and the Netherlands (mostly from Indonesia). In Spain a new mosque has recently been opened, the first since the fall of the last Muslim kingdoms five centuries ago. In south-eastern Europe, notably Yugoslavia, Albania and Greece, there are long-established Muslim communities whose origins date back to the Ottoman conquests of the fifteenth and sixteenth centuries.

See also *Education.*

Mysticism

See *Sufis.*

Pakistan

See *Ahmadiyya, Islam in South Asia, Muslims in Britain, Purdah.*

Pilgrimage

See *Hajj.*

Pillars of the Faith

All Muslims acknowledge the obligation to show their submission in terms of the five "Pillars of the Faith":

(A) profession of the creed (*shahada/kalima*): "I testify that there is no God but Allah, and that Muhammad is the Prophet of Allah." This formula is also recited into the ear of a new-born baby and is the basic expression of the fundamental belief that there is only *one* God, the creator and sustainer of the universe and judge of mankind.

(B) ritual prayer, preceded by an act of ablution (*wudu*), five times a day.

(C) the annual donation of a certain proportion of one's wealth for the use of the poor and disadvantaged, or for pious purposes, such as mosque-building or education. This is called *zakat* and is not a tax but a "purification" of wealth, through sharing.

(D) fasting (*saum*) throughout daylight hours, from sunrise to sunset, in the month of Ramadan.

(E) undertaking the pilgrimage to Mecca (the *hajj*).

Muslims are also forbidden pork, alcohol, gambling and usury and enjoined to honesty, fortitude and generosity. Strong family ties and respect for older relatives are marked characteristics of Muslim societies.

See also *Beliefs, Fasting, Hajj, Jihad, Prayer, Shahada, Zakat.*

The first pillar of Islam is Shahadah, which concerns belief in Tawhid and Risalah (prophethood) of Muhammad. The other four pillars make up Ibadah. Ibadah, an Arabic term, includes any activity which is done to gain Allah's favour. Salat (prayer), Zakat, Sawm (Fasting) and Hajj are the main forms of worship or Ibadah. If we perform them regularly and correctly, we come closer to Allah, our Creator and Sustainer.

These four basic duties of Salat, Zakat, Sawm and Hajj comprise the training programme which has been designed for us by Allah so that we can shape our life around Shahadah. We already know that we belong to Allah and He is our Master. So, in order to behave like the servant of our Creator, we must practise Salat, Zakat, Sawm and Hajj faithfully.

(Ghulam Sarwar, *Islam: Beliefs and Teachings*, Muslim Educational Trust, 1982)

Politics

In the western world it is customary to separate politics and religion. Politics, by definition, relate to public matters, whereas religion is a private concern. But this separation has only come about in recent centuries. In traditional Muslim countries, such as Saudi Arabia, politics and religion merge into one another because both are expressions of Islam, surrendering to the will of God. And in Islam the difference between public and private is meaningless. Muhammad himself was both a religious leader, concerned with teaching spiritual truth, and a political leader, responsible for organizing the community of believers. Islam favours no particular form of government over any other, but an Islamic state must have at least two characteristics. The first is that the laws are based on the Qur'an or at least do not contradict it. The second is that only Muslims can hold key positions of power. In practice, these conditions are not always fulfilled in many countries which have large Muslim populations.

See also *Caliphate, Dhimmi, Jihad, Mahdi, Medina, Muslim Brethren.*

Atatürk – "Father of the Turks". This statue, set up in ▷ the 1920s, was itself a challenge to traditional Muslim disapproval of "idols".

Protest poster, London.

Polygamy

See *Marriage*.

Prayer

Prayer (*salat*) is the core of Muslim worship. The Qur'an stresses its significance repeatedly: "Prayer at fixed times has been enjoined on the believers" (4:103). "Establish prayer to remember me" (20:14).

Prayer should be preceded by an announcement of intention (*niya*) to make an act of worship, so as to ensure the total sincerity and concentration of the worshipper and to prevent it from becoming an empty ritual.

Wherever they are in the world, Muslims always pray facing towards Mecca. At first, the direction (*qibla*) of prayer was towards Jerusalem, until later a revelation from Allah caused Muhammad to redirect Muslim devotions towards the site of the *Ka'ba*. In every mosque, the *qibla* is indicated by a niche (*mihrab*).

Men and women normally pray separately; indeed, in many Muslim countries, women only usually pray at home. Where men and women do use the same mosque, the women pray either beside, behind or above the men, depending on local custom.

Muslims should pray five times a day. The first prayer (*fajr*) is offered between first light and sunrise; the second (*zuhr*) after midday; the third (*asr*) after mid-afternoon; the fourth (*maghrib*) after sunset; and the fifth (*isha*) after dark. The exact time will vary according to the latitude and local conditions. Muslims should not pray at the actual times of sunrise, noon and sunset. This no doubt symbolizes Islam's rejection of pagan sun-worship.

Prayers are preceded by an act of ritual ablution (*wudu*). They may be offered in any clean place, not necessarily in a mosque. However, Muslims are encouraged to pray together, rather than alone. On Fridays, around midday, adult male Muslims should, if possible, go to the mosque to offer

Prayers to mark the end of Ramadan in Senegal.

prayers as part of a congregation. On such occasions it is usual for the *imam* to preach a sermon. But the prime duty of the *imam* is to lead the prayers of the faithful who line up in rows behind him.

Shoes are not worn during the ritual prayer and the head is usually covered. Prayer rugs (*sajjada*) are often used but are not essential. Muslims offer their prayers in Arabic, whatever their own first language.

The words of prayer (praise for Allah and Muhammad and a recitation of the first chapter of the Qur'an) and the gestures (*rak'a*, literally "bending") used are modelled on the example of the Prophet. They both proclaim and symbolize the humble submission of the believer before Allah. The number of *rak'as* is usually four, except for the first prayer, when there are two, and the fourth prayer, when there are three.

In addition to the set daily prayers in Arabic, Muslims are permitted to say their own personal prayers (*du'a*), for asking, thanking and adoring, in their own language. During Ramadan, during festivals and when seeking success in a venture or journey, Muslims are also encouraged to offer extra prayers. Rhythmic chants (*dhikr*), based on the name of God, are an important part of *sufi* devotions.

See also *Ablution, al-Fatiha, Funerals, Imam, Khutba, Mosque, Qibla.*

Prophets

Muslims believe that, since the beginning of the world, Allah has sent prophets to every people, to communicate His teachings to Man. Prophets, according to Islam, are human and not divine, though Muslim tradition later asserted that they were without sin, and popular folklore attributed many miraculous deeds to them. A saying of the Prophet declares that there have been 124,000 prophets, the last being Muhammad himself. Of these 124,000 prophets, most are considered as *nabi* (plural: *anbiya*), but 315, including 25 mentioned by name in the Qur'an (6:83-6), are regarded as having the status of *rasul* (plural: *rusul*) or "messenger", because they have been sent to a specific community, with a scripture and a code of divine law to guide it (10:48; 14:4).

See also *Abraham, Ahmadiyya, Black Muslims, Jesus, Muhammad.*

> *We sent Messengers before thee; of some We have related to thee, and some We have not related to thee. It was not for any Messenger to bring a sign, save by God's leave. When God's command comes, justly the issue shall be decided; then the vain-doers shall be lost.*
>
> *The Believers (40:77)*

Purdah

This is the custom of secluding women from contact with adult men, other than their closest relatives. The word is Persian in origin (as the custom itself may be) and means "curtain" or "screen" and hence is applied to the custom of veiling and wearing long enveloping garments (*burqa, chador*) as well as to the seclusion of women in private apartments (*harem*). The Qur'an requires neither of these practices, although it does require women – and men – to dress and behave modestly. Nevertheless, *purdah* has been widely observed until the twentieth century and still is in some parts of Pakistan and in Saudi Arabia. It has also been reinstated among some Muslims concerned at the spread of western influences, most noticeably in Iran. In most village communities it has been difficult to uphold a complete system of *purdah*, especially among the poor, but in the towns and among the better-off it has been more practicable. Women have not necessarily been isolated from one another by their seclusion from men, for they are able to meet in one another's houses, at the village well and in the *hammam* (bath-house).

See also *Dress, Women.*

Qibla

The direction in which Muslims face when offering their prayers. This is commonly said to be Mecca but more accurately is the *Ka'ba* itself. In a mosque the *qibla* is indicated by the *mihrab*, an empty niche set in the wall which faces in the appropriate direction. Travellers often carry a compass, to help them find the correct *qibla* when they cannot get to a mosque.

See also *Astronomy, Ka'ba, Mosque.*

Chinese Muslims kneel before the *mihrab*, the niche which indicates the *qibla*.

al-Quds

See *Jerusalem.*

Qur'an

Sometimes written "Koran", the Qur'an is the sacred scripture of Islam. The literal meaning of the word is "recitation", because it consists of the collected pronouncements of the Prophet Muhammad. Muslims do *not* regard Muhammad as the author of the Qur'an because the words are held to be the actual speech of Allah. Muhammad was simply the vehicle through which God chose to speak to humanity and this is reflected in the way in which some passages of the Qur'an are addressed to believers, some to unbelievers and some simply to Muhammad himself.

The Qur'an is roughly as long as the New Testament and is divided into 114 chapters, known as *suras*, each of which has a name, usually relating to its initial word or some theme or incident in it.

A Qur'an stand, inlaid with gold and mother-of-pearl.

Suras vary in length from two lines to over seven hundred. The *suras* are not arranged in the chronological order in which they were revealed to Muhammad but in the order given them when they were collected together and written down on the orders of the Caliph Uthman (644-56). The first chapter, *al-Fatiha* (The Opening), is recited by devout Muslims every day as part of their prayers. It is followed by a number of long *suras* which give practical details on the running of the Muslim community, such as rules for divorce and inheritance. These were revealed after the *hijra*, when the Prophet was organizing the first group of believers in Medina. The early *suras*, revealed in Mecca at the beginning of his prophetic career, follow these and are shorter and more lyrical and deal with abstract questions of belief, death, judgment and the afterlife. Most scholars agree that *Sura* 96, the "Blood Clot", was the first to be revealed; it is usually supposed that this took place on the "Night of Power" which is usually dated as the 27th day of Ramadan.

The style of the Qur'an depends upon rhythm rather than rhyme. It is taken to be the standard of excellence against which all other Arabic writing is judged. When sceptics challenged Muhammad to

Recitation from the Qur'an at the opening of a new Muslim school in London.

The Qur'an is also for silent study and meditation.

work miracles to prove that he was a Prophet, he simply referred them to his divinely inspired utterances and challenged them to devise anything half so powerful and elegant. Poets, it must be remembered, were among the most respected members of Arab tribal society, for they sang the praises of warriors, women, ancestors and horses. It was therefore altogether fitting that the praises of a creator God should be expressed in a style even more exalted than anything that had preceded it or was to come.

The Qur'an is regarded by Muslims as the final and complete revelation from God. Other scriptures, such as the *Torah* and Gospels, are regarded as valid but inadequate, having been, from the Muslim point of view, distorted or corrupted since they were first received from God. Special care is taken, therefore, to preserve the Qur'an from the slightest alteration, both in the way it is written or printed and in the way in which it is recited. Strictly speaking, the Qur'an cannot be translated, although versions for purposes of study rather than worship exist in all the world's major languages.

The making of beautiful Qur'ans has long been a supreme expression of the arts of calligraphy and book-binding. The Qur'an is always treated with the greatest respect, raised on a stand when being read aloud and wrapped in a cloth or stored in a high place when not in use. While the Qur'an is being read aloud, a devout Muslim should neither smoke, speak nor eat. Each year in Malaysia nowadays an international Qur'an reading contest is organized.

The Qur'an is regarded therefore as humanity's basic source of guidance for living. It is the inspiration for law and literature, and for manners as well as morals. Not surprisingly, knowledge of the Qur'an lay at the core of traditional Islamic education and many Muslims, both in the past and in the present, have managed to learn the whole of it by heart, thus earning the valued title of "*hafiz*".

See also *Arabic Language, Education, al-Fatiha, Hadith, Law, Muhammad.*

Race

See *Black Muslims, Hajj, Umma.*

Ramadan

See *Fasting.*

Saudi Arabia

See *Hajj, Purdah, Wahhabis.*

Science

See *Astronomy, Education, Ibn Sina.*

Shahada

This profession of belief (also known as the *kalima*) is the first "pillar of the faith" and sums up the Muslim's creed in a single sentence – "*La ilaha illal Lah, Muhammadur Rasulullah*" ("There is no god but Allah and Muhammad is the Prophet of Allah"). This declaration, in the form of beautiful calligraphy, has often been used for decoration in art and architecture.

See also *Allah, Beliefs, Muhammad, Pillars of the Faith.*

... the Muslim community symbolizes its belief in probably the simplest, tidiest creed in all the world.... The Muslims themselves refer to this simply as 'the two words' or even 'the word'.... To repeat this creed is, formally, to become a Muslim; perhaps to understand it, is to understand a Muslim (Wilfred Cantwell Smith, *The Faith of Other Men*, Canadian Broadcasting Corporation Publications, 1962)

Shari'a

See *Law.*

Shi'ites

Between 85 and 90% of Muslims are Sunnite, followers of the *sunna* (way of the Prophet). The remaining Shi'ite minority take their name from the *Shi'at Ali*, the followers of Ali, son-in-law of the Prophet. They regard Ali, and his descendants, as the true heirs of Muhammad's position as rightful leader of the Muslim community.

The distinction between Sunnite and Shi'ite goes back to the violent struggle over political power, which resulted in the death of Ali in 661. It developed over the years, to give rise to differences of doctrine, ritual and religious style. Shi'ism, with its emphasis on sacrifice and martyrdom and its belief in an inner, hidden meaning in the Qur'an, has generated various traditions of belief and practice. Shi'ites pay particular reverence to the sites associated with the deaths of Ali and his sons (in Iraq) and special importance is accorded to the 10th of Muharram, the anniversary of their martyrdom.

Only in Iran is Shi'ism the dominant form of Islam. Although Shi'ism is not the established religion, Shi'ites also constitute a majority in Iraq and significant and well-organized minorities in the Gulf, East Africa, Pakistan and India.

In non-Muslim societies, such as Britain, the distinction between Sunnite and Shi'ite is, of course, felt to be less significant than the difference between Muslim and non-Muslim.

See also *Ali, Imam, Isma'ilis, Law, Mahdi, Sunna*.

Indian flagellants mourn the deaths of Husayn and Hasan on the 10th of Muharram.

Slavery

The Qur'an bids masters to treat slaves kindly and encourages them to set them free, one of the purposes for which *zakat* may be used. In the medieval period slaves were often able to reach powerful positions in the army or at court. Slave trading also provided one of the important links between the Arab world and Africa. Nowadays, slavery is said to survive in some parts of West Africa and the Arabian Peninsula, although it was formally abolished in Saudi Arabia in 1962.

See also *Africa, Zakat*.

Sufis

Since the early days of Islam, some Muslims have sought to draw themselves ever closer to God. These mystics are known as *sufis*, from the simple woollen garment (*suf*) they usually wore to show

A group of Sudanese *sufis*.

Tomb of a *sufi* shaikh of the Mevlana order, Konya, Turkey.

that they didn't care about wealth and fashion. *Sufis* developed special techniques, such as rhythmic prayer, breathing or movement, to bring upon themselves a sense of immediate oneness with God. Some, like Jalal al-Din Rumi, the thirteenth-century Persian mystic, wrote beautiful poetry, expressing their joy in God and his Creation. Many founded orders (*tariqa* – literally "roads") of organized followers who accepted the guidance and example of the founding *shaikh* (literally, "old man"). Numbers of these orders, such as the Qadiriyya and Tijanniya, have been very influential in spreading Islam beyond the Arab lands, and flourish to this day, although they have at various times drawn the disapproval of more conventional Muslims. In areas where the *sufi* orders have been traditionally strong, such as North Africa and South Asia, even Muslims who do not belong to them have great respect for their *shaikhs*, as teachers, healers and settlers of disputes.

See also *Fasting, Folk Religion, al-Ghazzali, Holy Men, Prayer.*

60

Sunna

Literally meaning "custom" or "manner", the *sunna* is the code of behaviour, based on Muhammad's example, as recorded in the *hadith*. About 85% of all Muslims are Sunni Muslims, following this general tradition, as distinct from the various Shi'ite groups, who are guided more directly by the teachings of their *Imams* and *mujtahids*.

See also *Hadith, Imam, Law, 'Ulama*.

'Ulama

Also spelt " *'ulema* ", this word literally means "learned men" and refers to those experts on the Qur'an, *hadith* and law who have traditionally administered justice and advised governments in Muslim countries. Generally speaking, they have been opponents of social change, especially where it has been associated with foreign influences. They have also voiced popular resistance to abuses of power from time to time – for instance, by withholding the customary praise for a ruler in the Friday *khutba* or refusing to administer justice in the courts. In the modern period their influence has tended to diminish under the impact of secular education, the adoption of western-style legal systems and the reduction of *waqf* lands on which many depended for their incomes. The Shi'ite equivalent of *'ulama* are *mujtahids*, from whose ranks *ayatullahs* emerge.

See also *Ayatullah, Education, Khutba, Law, Politics, Waqf*.

> . . . Islam has no clergy and no orthodoxy in the Christian sense. There is no pope, no bishops or bishoprics, no hierarchy, and no councils or synods to determine and impose an approved creed and to condemn deviations from it as heterodoxy. Such authorities were never constituted in Islam, and the few attempts to do so failed utterly. The ulema are men of religious learning, not priests; they receive no ordination, have no parishes and perform no sacraments.
> (Bernard Lewis, *Islam from the Prophet Muhammad to the Capture of Constantinople*, Macmillan, 1974)

Umayyads

See *Caliphate*.

Umma

Originally used to describe Muhammad's followers in Medina, this word is now used to describe the world-wide community of all Muslims, whose unity in belief should transcend all national boundaries and ethnic differences.

Veiling

See *Purdah*.

Wahhabis

A conservative reform movement begun by Muhammad bin 'Abd al-Wahhab (1703-92), who opposed such customs as the veneration of the tombs of so-called holy men, the use of rosaries in prayer and other practices which had developed over the centuries. He called instead for a return to the rigour and simplicity of early Islam. The Wahhabi cause was taken up by the Saudi family who eventually conquered and united most of the Arabian peninsula under their rule (1932). Continuing Wahhabi influence also ensures continuing resistance in Saudi Arabia to western influences, such as the drinking of alcohol, which is tolerated in other Muslim countries.

See also *Folk Religion*.

Waqf

A pious endowment, usually a gift of land, the income from which is used to support a worthy institution such as a mosque, college or hospital. *Waqf* could also be established for the benefit of one's family. Being exempt from taxation and seizure by governments, *waqf* (plural *awqaf*) was an attractive way of conserving private wealth. In some ways it was therefore similar to the sort of entail arrangement used by landowning families in England to prevent their estates being sold or broken up. In modern times most governments in Muslim countries have regulated the use of *waqf* lands to ensure that the income they produce is put to proper purposes and they are not simply a means of tax avoidance.

See also *'Ulama*.

War

See *Jihad*.

Wealth

The right to own private property is firmly recognized in Islam, but great differences of wealth and poverty in a community are deplored, as is oppression or neglect of the poor by the wealthy. *Zakat* offers the Muslim a way to "purify his wealth" by applying part of it to God's purposes. Loaning money at interest is strictly forbidden to Muslims, as is gambling, but profits can be taken from ventures involving an element of risk. Some Muslim authorities disapprove of insurance, on the grounds that it seeks to thwart the consequences of God's will.

See also *Waqf, Zakat*.

> To seek lawful gain is the duty of every Muslim. He who ends the day weary from the work of his hands ends the day forgiven for his sins. The honest, truthful Muslim merchant will stand with the martyrs on the Day of Judgment.
> (Sayings attributed to the Prophet Muhammad)

Women

The teachings of the Qur'an represented a great advance in the position of women in Arabian society, granting them rights of property and inheritance and forbidding the common practice of female infanticide. While confirming the spiritual equality of men and women, the Qur'an also confirmed the authority of husbands over wives (4:34). Special allowance is made for women in respect of certain religious obligations. While menstruating they are excused prayers and fasting; days missed from fasting must be made up later,

> A virtuous wife is a man's best treasure. The most perfect Muslims are those whose disposition is best; and the best of you are they who behave best with their wives. Paradise lies at the feet of mothers.
> (Sayings attributed to the Prophet Muhammad)

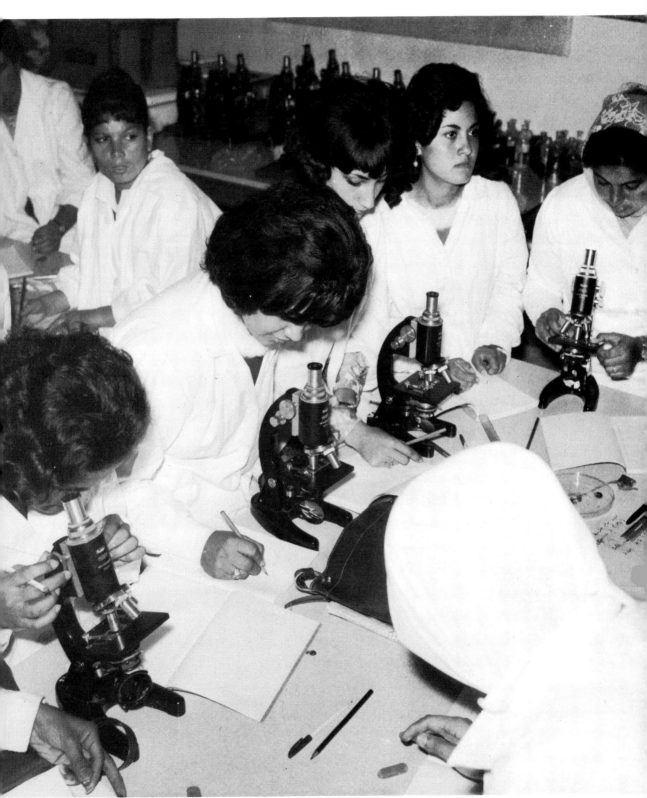

Women scientists at al-Azhar university, Cairo.

but prayers need not be. Women are also excused attendance at Friday prayers at the mosque. When women pray in the mosques it is usual for them to be behind or beside the men or in a separate part. In modern times the governments of Muslim countries have made much greater efforts than was usual in traditional communities to ensure that women receive the benefits of education. Famous Muslim women of the past include the Prophet's wives, Khadija and Aisha, his daughter Fatima and the mystic *sufi* poet Rabia.

See also *Circumcision, Divorce, Dress, Education, Marriage, Purdah.*

Wudu

See *Ablution.*

Zakat

Each year, at the end of Ramadan, Muslims must pay *zakat* by making over a certain amount of their wealth for the benefit of the poor and needy. Muslims insist that *zakat* is neither a tax payment nor a charitable donation. A charitable gift is optional, *zakat* is not. A tax may be spent on any purpose, but the ways in which *zakat* can be spent are detailed in the Qur'an (9:60). Muslims regard the payment of *zakat* as an act of worship (*ibadah*), just like prayer. In praying, the Muslim uses voice, mind and body to express praise and obedience; *zakat* enables the believer to use wealth for the same purpose. Throughout the Qur'an, prayer and *zakat* are linked as twin obligations for the true believer (2:277; 31:2-4; 98:5).

The word *zakat* means "purify" and is also sometimes translated as "sweeten" or "cleanse". It suggests the idea that, by making over part of his wealth for the needs of others, the believer purifies his right to the rest and protects himself from the dangers of greed and selfishness. It also shows the believer's acceptance that all wealth really belongs to Allah, and that the owner is merely a trustee who will be judged by the way he has used it (27:60). Payment of *zakat* is therefore a religious duty (*fard*) for those who have wealth, and receipt of *zakat* is a positive right for those who do not. Ideally, *zakat* should prevent hoarding (59:7) and enable the Muslim community to avoid the tensions which arise from extremes of poverty and wealth.

The actual amount to be paid in *zakat* is subject to complicated rules. *Zakat* is payable on wealth in the form of gold and silver, cash and bank deposits, crops and herds, minerals and merchandise, but not on houses, clothes, furniture, machinery or

All wealth and riches belong to God. It is entrusted to us by Him, so that We may satisfy our needs and help our less fortunate brothers to satisfy their requirements. Thus the object of poor due is, first, to prove our faithfulness to our Master by making material sacrifice in obedience to His Command and for His Pleasure; second, to help the poorer section of the community to meet their basic needs without any hardship and inconvenience, in the best possible way; third, to achieve equitable distribution of wealth, along with the operation of the law of inheritance and the zero rate of interest, so that no one in the community is deprived of its benefits. Bot the rich and the poor share the social wealth for the satisfaction of their needs. Islam wants every man and woman to live in honour and dignity. It wants to build up the community on very strong moral and economic foundations so that it can survive against all opposition. It can never tolerate poverty amid plenty. . . . The institution of zakat is meant to correct such a situation and, instead, to establish a right and just balance between the two extremes. . . . In short the institution of zakat purifies individuals as well as society and increases goodness in every heart. . . . (Afzalur Rahman, *Islam: Ideology and the Way of Life*, Muslim Schools Trust, 1980)

tools. A believer must have held the wealth for a whole year to be liable to pay *zakat* on it and there is a bottom level (*nisab*) for each commodity, below which its possessor is exempt (e.g. 5 camels or 40 goats). For cash, the lowest usual rate is 2½% of the year's savings. It is up to the Muslim's own conscience how much he or she chooses to pay above this level. Women and children as well as men are liable to pay *zakat*, if they have sufficient wealth; *zakat* is also the first charge on a dead person's estate, even before debts are paid off.

Zakat is to be paid to those who are too poor to support themselves or their families; to those who have lost their wealth through disaster or ill-fortune; to debtors, captives and travellers in distress; to the officials who arrange its collection and distribution; and to uphold the faith by providing scholarships for students or helping converts to Islam or even by buying weapons for defence. In the past, the *zakat* system was organized by the state. Nowadays, and especially in non-Muslim countries, it is usually a matter of voluntary organization. Payment of *zakat* does not exempt Muslims from making voluntary contributions (*sadaqa*) for good causes, preferably in secret (2:264 ; 3:92).

See also *Slavery, Wealth.*

---

*And perform the prayer, and pay the alms,
and lend to God a good loan. Whatever
good you shall forward to your souls'
account, you shall find it with God as Better,
and mightier a wage. And ask
God's forgiveness: God is All-forgiving,
All-compassionate.*

Enwrapped (73:19)

Date List

AH		AD/CE
52 years before H.	Birth of the Prophet	c.570
27 years before H.	Marriage with Khadija	c.595
12/13 years before H.	First experience of the Qur'an	609-10
7 years before H.	First Muslims find refuge in Ethiopia	615
3 years before H.	Death of Khadija and of Abu Talib, Muhammad's protector	619
–	The Hijra	622
2	Muhammad's victory at Badr	624
3	Muhammad's reverse at Uhud	625
8	Conquest of Mecca and consolidation of Islam	630
11	Death of Muhammad	632
13	Death of Abu Bakr, the first Caliph	634
13/15	Capture of Damascus and Jerusalem	636/37
18/19	Conquest of Egypt and Persia	639/40
23	Murder of Umar, the second Caliph	644
29	Canon of the Qur'an established	c.650
35	Murder of Uthman, the third Caliph	656
40	Assassination of Ali, the fourth Caliph	661
61	Massacre of Karbala and death of Husain	680
71/72	Construction of the Dome of the Rock, Jerusalem and of the the al-Aqsa Mosque	690/91
92	Muslims under Tariq cross from Morocco into Spain	711
94	Entry into Indus Valley	713
94	Taking of Cordoba, Spain	713
95	Capture of Samarqand	714
110	Death of Hasan al-Basri, earliest known *sufi*	728
114	Battle of Tours: Turn of the tide of Islam in France	732
132	Rise of the Abbasid Caliphate	750
145	Foundation of Baghdad by Caliph al-Mansur	762
148	*Imam* of the "Seveners" goes into "hiddenness"	765
193	Death of Harun al-Rashid of the Abbasid "golden age"	809
264	*Imam* of the "Twelvers" goes into "hiddenness"	878
492	Crusaders capture Jerusalem	1099
564	Accession to power of Salah al-Din (Saladin)	1169
657	Sack of Baghdad by the Mongols and fall of the Abbasid Caliphate	1258
859	Ottoman Turks capture Constantinople	1453
897	Fall of Granada: end of Muslim Spain	1492
923	Selim I conquers Egypt and carries the last titular Abbasid Caliph to Istanbul	1517

927-74	Sulaiman the Magnificent, greatest of the Ottomans	1520-66
971	Akbar, greatest of the Mughals, comes to power	1563
1119	Death of Aurangzeb, decline of Mughal India	1707
1213	Napoleon in Egypt	1798
1246	French occupation of Algeria	1830
1274	Indian rebellion against British rule	1857
1286	Suez Canal completed	1869
1298	British occupation of Egypt	1881
1320	Qasim Amin pioneers Egyptian feminism	1902
1325	"Young Turks" in Istanbul and new "liberalism"	1908
1330f.	Beginnings of oil-prospecting in Persia	1910-11
1342	Abolition of the Caliphate and secularization of Turkey under Ataturk	1924
1347	Founding of the Muslim Brotherhood by Hasan al-Banna	1928
1366	Partition of India and creation of Pakistan	1947
1366	UN vote partitioning Palestine and creation of the State of Israel	1947
1386	Israeli occupation of Jerusalem, West Jordan and Sinai	1967
1391	East Pakistan leaves West Pakistan and becomes Bangla-Desh	1971
1393	Organization of Petroleum Exporting Countries (OPEC) quadruples oil price Arab-Israeli War	1973
1395	Civil war breaks out in Lebanon	1975
1396	World of Islam Festival in Britain	1976
1397	First Muslim World Education Conference General Zia takes power in Pakistan	1977
1398	Marxist coup in Afghanistan	1978
1399	Pahlavi dynasty overthrown in Iran	1979
1400	Armed attack on the Great Mosque at Mecca Iran-Iraq war breaks out	1980

Useful Addresses

Association of British Muslims,
92 Stapleton Hall Road,
London N4

The Centre for the Study of Islam and Christian-Muslim Relations,
Selly Oak Colleges,
Birmingham B29 6LE

Commission for Racial Equality,
10-12 Allington Street,
London SW1

The Institute of Isma'ili Studies,
14-15 Great James Street,
London WC1N 3DP

The Islamic Centre,
2A Sutherland Street,
Leicester LE2 1DS

The Islamic Cultural Centre,
146 Park Road (off Baker Street),
London NW8

The Islamic Foundation,
233 London Road,
Leicester LE2 1ZE

The London Mosque,
16 Gressenhall Road,
London SW18

The Muslim Educational Trust,
130 Strand Green Road,
London N4 3RZ

The Muslim Schools Trust,
78 Gillespie Road,
London N5 1LN

The Muslim World League,
46 Goodge Street,
London W1

Muslim Youth Association,
31 Draycott Place,
London SW3

The UK Islamic Mission,
202 North Gower Street,
London NW1 2LY

Union of Muslim Organizations of the UK and Eire,
30 Baker Street,
London W1M 2DS

Books for Further Reading

The Arab World Today Richard Tames (Kaye & Ward, 1980)

The Buildings of Early Islam Helen and Richard Leacroft (Hodder & Stoughton, 1976)

Egypt Michael van Haag (Macdonald Educational, 1975)

India and Pakistan in the Twentieth Century Richard Tames (Batsford, 1981)

Islam: Beliefs & Teachings Ghulam Sarwar (The Muslim Educational Trust, 1982)

Islam for Children Ahmad von Denffer (The Islamic Foundation, 1981)

The Middle East Maureen Abdullah (Macdonald Educational, 1980)

The Middle East in the Twentieth Century Richard I. Lawless (Batsford, 1980)

The Moors Gerald Hawting (Sampson Low, 1978)

The Muslim World Richard Tames (Macdonald Educational, 1982)

The Oil States W.B. Fisher (Batsford, 1980)

The Religious Dimension: Islam Riadh El-Droubie & Edward Hulmes (Longman, 1980)

The Rise of Islam Anton Powell (Longman, 1979)

Turkey David Hotham (Macdonald Educational, 1975)

Books for Reference

Abingdon Dictionary of Living Religions Keith Crim (ed.) (Abingdon, 1981)

Approaches to Islam Richard Tames (John Murray, 1982)

The Arabs Peter Mansfield (Penguin, 1978)

Architecture of the Islamic World George Michell (ed.) (Thames & Hudson, 1978)

The Arts of Islam Titus Burckhardt (World of Islam Festival Trust, 1976)

A Dictionary of Comparative Religion S.G.F. Brandon (ed.) (Weidenfeld & Nicolson, 1970)

Introduction to Islam Muhammad Hamidullah (MWH London Publishers, 1979)

Islam H.A.R. Gibb (Oxford University Press, 2nd edition, 1968)

Islam: A Westerner's Guide D.S. Roberts (Kogan Page, 1981)

Islam: Ideology and Way of Life Afzalur Rahman (The Muslim Schools Trust, 1980)

Islam in the World Malise Ruthven (Penguin, 1984)

The Legacy of Islam J. Schacht & C.E. Bosworth (ed.) (Oxford University Press, 1974)

The Muslim Guide Mustafa Yusuf McDermott (The Islamic Foundation, 1980)

The Muslim Mind Charis Waddy (Longman, 1976)

Muslim Peoples: A World Ethnographic Survey Richard V. Weekes (ed.) (Greenwood Press, 1978)

The Penguin Dictionary of Religions John R. Hinnells (ed.) (Penguin, 1984)

The Spread of Islam Michael Rogers (Phaidon, 1976)

The World of Islam Bernard Lewis (ed.) (Thames & Hudson, 1976)

Index